CW01424976

STEAMING INTO
NORTHAMPTONSHIRE

Frontispiece
'The Thames-Clyde Express', pride of the Midland line, leans on the curve at the south end of Kettering station with Saltley Black 5 No. 44805, impatient for a prompt 5.48 p.m. departure for St. Pancras in 1959.
(L. W. Roy)

STEAMING INTO NORTHAMPTONSHIRE

compiled by RICHARD COLEMAN and JOE RAJCZONEK

NORTHAMPTONSHIRE LIBRARIES

This book is dedicated to Northamptonshire's Railwaymen

Published by
Northamptonshire Libraries,
27 Guildhall Road,
Northampton NN1 1EF.

Published 1988 Reprinted 1989

© 1988 Text Copyright
Northamptonshire
Libraries, Richard Coleman
and Joe Rajczonek.
ISBN: 0 905391 12 8

Designed by
Bernard Crossland

Typeset in Century and
printed in Great Britain by
Stanley L. Hunt (Printers) Ltd.
Midland Road, Rushden

CAPTIONS

Half title
An Aspinall ex-L. & Y. R. 'Pug' No. 11212, on loan to Northampton Borough Engineer's Department, stands in the West Bridge Depot yard, summer 1934.
(W. J. S. Meredith)

Title page
Cyclist, bus driver and photographer alike get the briefest glimpse of Princess Royal Pacific No. 6206 PRINCESS MARIE LOUISE, then less than a month old, racing northwards over the A43 at Blisworth, with the down 'Royal Scot' on 16 September 1935.
(W. J. S. Meredith)

Front end-papers
The first Northampton Castle station was no more than a large halt, and is seen here with a platelayers' train circa 1876. The train is being hauled by a Crewe modernised, Wolverton built, McConnell 0-4-2 goods engine of 1862 vintage. Foreman-platelayer George Webb, standing beside the locomotive, came to Northampton in 1869 for the then princely sum of 16/- per week.
(L. Hanson collection)

The construction of the southern extension to the Great Central Railway was nearing completion in the late 1890s. Special guests celebrate the occasion by posing in an open wagon, behind Manning Wardle 0-6-0 CICETER, in the vicinity of Brackley.
(Courtesy Mrs. D. Pengelly)

Back end-papers
Only two locomotives carried names linked with Northamptonshire. Great Western County class No. 1022 COUNTY OF NORTHAMPTON seen here at Hatton bank, Budbrooke on Saturday, 12 January 1957, and L.M.S. Royal Scot class No. 6147 THE NORTHAMPTONSHIRE REGIMENT, photographed in typical official pose on 21 November 1935.
(T. E. Williams and The Derby collection, courtesy N.R.M. York)

Thompson B1 class No. 61156 storms over the twenty arch, 320 feet long Brackley viaduct, as it heads south with the 'South Yorkshireman' during March 1950.
(Betty Hutchings A.R.P.S.)

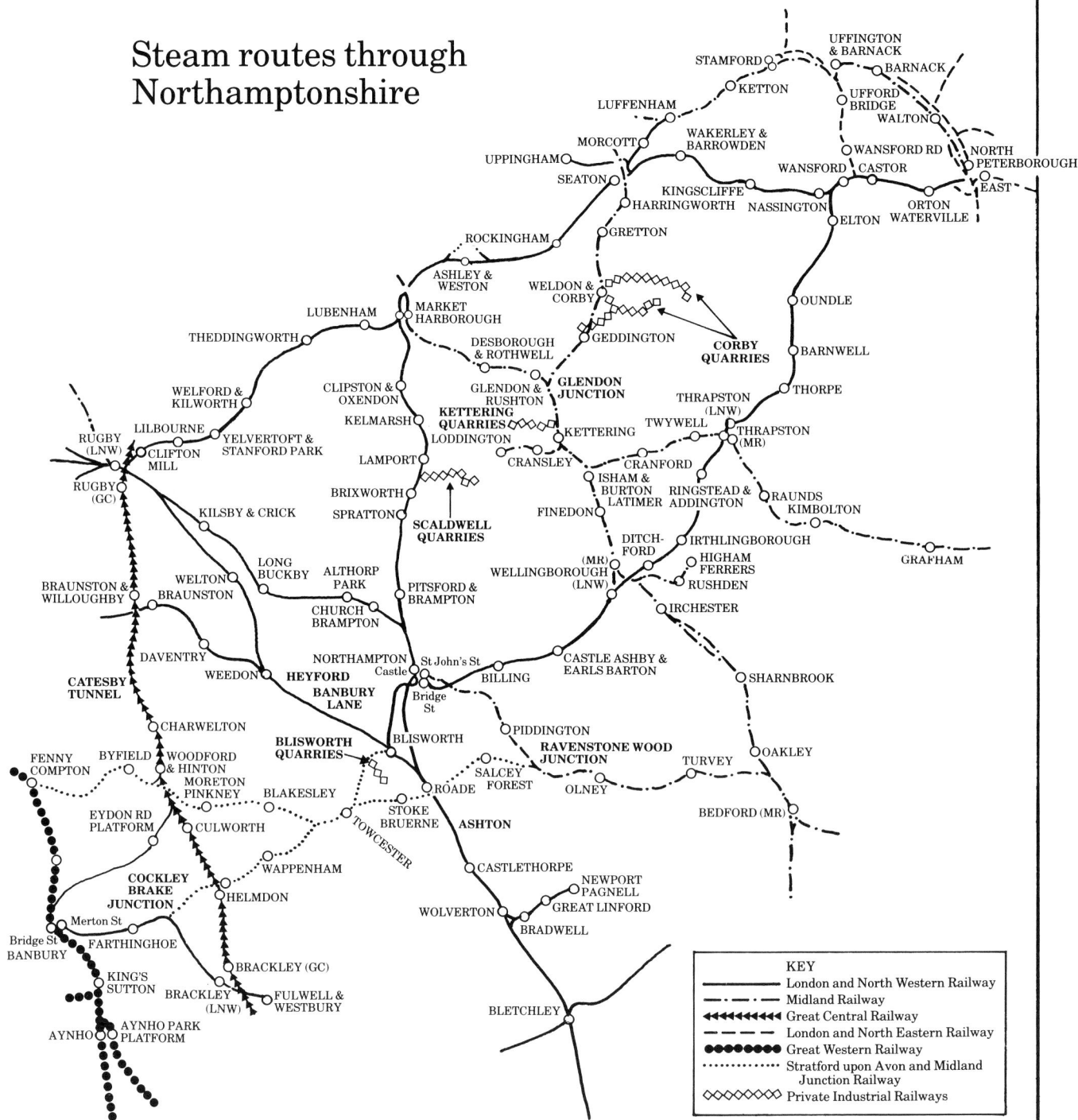

Steam routes through Northamptonshire

KEY
————————	London and North Western Railway
–·–·–·–·–	Midland Railway
◄◄◄◄◄◄◄◄◄	Great Central Railway
– – – – –	London and North Eastern Railway
●●●●●●●●	Great Western Railway
··············	Stratford upon Avon and Midland Junction Railway
◇◇◇◇◇◇◇	Private Industrial Railways

INTRODUCTION

In our book *Steam Nostalgia around Northampton* we attempted to rekindle in the minds of readers happy memories of the past, as they browsed through the pages covering Northampton and its immediate surrounding area during the days of the steam locomotive.

From the comments and letters we received it is satisfying to know of the pleasure it gave to so many people, the only complaint being that in some cases 'their part of the County had been missed out'.

In this companion volume we have attempted to rectify this as much as possible, even reaching outside the County boundary where necessary, to enhance the interest of that particular line or section. Consequently the coverage of Northampton itself has been slightly reduced in an effort to give an overall balance to the two volumes.

It is virtually impossible to cover every location and the final choice, as before, has been decided by the interest, atmosphere and quality of the photographs available.

The County was fortunate to be represented by so many railway companies. The ex-London and North Western and Midland (L.M.S.) main lines and branches predominated, while the Great Central route ran along the western boundary. A glimpse of the Great Western could be obtained at the south-western tip, and the London and North Eastern appropriately traversed the north-eastern corner through the Soke of Peterborough. Lastly the Stratford-upon-Avon and Midland Junction, whose lines meandered their way across the County.

Northamptonshire also supported a comprehensive network of industrial lines, particularly around the Corby and Kettering areas, for the excavation of iron ore. We felt it appropriate, therefore, to include a small number of photographs which, it is hoped, will give a brief insight into the character of these privately owned byways.

The majority of the photographs are previously unpublished, and have been selected and printed from the collections of some forty photographers.

May you derive much pleasure browsing through this selection of steam scenes from a bygone age when, for many people, a trip by train was something special.

Richard Coleman and Joe Rajczonek

CONTENTS

ACKNOWLEDGMENTS

Once again we are indebted to all the many photographers who have so kindly allowed us access to their unique collections of photographs. Also to John Meredith for the loan of his father's negatives and to W. G. Allen for the use of the late L. J. Thompson's photographs. Without their superb pictures this book would never have been possible.

Thanks must also be attributed to Messrs. Peter Butler, Chris Clayson, Bryan Cross, Ken Fairey, Tony Foster, Ron Gammage, A. E. Grigg, David Hanson, Victor A. Hatley, John Morrison, Norman Oldfield, Robin Puryer, Patrick Rawlinson, Tim Shuttleworth, Ian L. Wright, Dave Wellington, B.R. signalman Maurice Coleman and driver Mike Winnett, the Northampton branch of the R.C.T.S. and the staff of the National Railway Museum Library, for much help and advice.

A special word of thanks must go to Les Hanson, Tony Heighton and Ross Smith who not only made their negatives available but spent many hours of their own time researching information for our needs. Also we must not forget to thank ex-Northampton steam driver Joe Hasdell for his invaluable knowledge and tales of the working railway in the days of steam.

Finally Northamptonshire Libraries have again given us great freedom in the choice of photographs during the preparation of the book for which we are extremely grateful, as we are to Robin Leleux from whom we have received generous co-operation.

THE PREMIER LINE

EUSTON: BLETCHLEY TO RUGBY

1. Euston's famous Doric Arch on Sunday, 17 August 1947. This imposing entrance greeted the traveller to the Premier Line for their journey northwards from the metropolis. (*W. J. S. Meredith*)

2. That wonderful railway aroma from the days of the steam locomotive, lingers in the haze under the station roof as Fowler Patriot No. 45519 LADY GODIVA blasts her train of red and cream coaches out of Euston, and heads for the County on Saturday, 20 June 1953. *(Geoff Rixon)*

THE PREMIER LINE   BLETCHLEY TO RUGBY

Opposite: 3. We re-join the Premier line at Bletchley in L.M.S. days with this superb aerial panorama taken on 26 April 1938. The line to Oxford curves out behind the carriage sheds at the top right, while the Bedford and Cambridge line curves out bottom left. At the end of the 1950s these two branches were linked by a concrete flyover. *(Aerofilms Ltd.)*

Below: 4. A miserable wet day at Bletchley finds two veteran ex-L.N.W.R. engines waiting to depart in the form of Webb 2-4-2 tank No. 6687 and Precursor 4-4-0 No. 25245 ANTAEUS on 30 October 1937. But hold on! ANTAEUS is carrying the name MAR-QUIS; a check back in the *Railway Observer* reveals all. ANTAEUS and MARQUIS had just been in Crewe works for overhaul and during refit the names were fixed to the wrong engines. Within a matter of days the MARQUIS nameplates were removed, and she ran nameless for some three months before being re-united with her correct ones. *(L. Hanson)*

5. The air is heavy with sulphur, kept down by the persistent fog at Bletchley station. Fowler Patriot No. 45548 LYTHAM ST. ANNE'S gives a long blast on its shrill whistle, temporarily deafening the gentleman onlooker, then heads away with her Euston to Blackpool express on 22 December 1956. *(Ross Smith)*

THE PREMIER LINE: BLETCHLEY TO RUGBY

6. Fowler Patriot No. 45503 THE ROYAL LEICESTERSHIRE REGIMENT receives attention to its live steam injector while standing at the south end of Bletchley station, having just arrived with the 12.11 p.m. train from Rugby to Euston at the end of May 1959. The large letter 'C' on the sign at this time indicated the start of a speed restriction; this would have been for the concrete flyover under construction at the time. The end of the speed restriction would have been indicated with a letter 'T'. *(P. I. Rawlinson)*

Left: 7. The engine crewman wipes the grime from his hands after preparing Ivatt 2-6-2 tank No. 41222 for its 5.42 p.m. departure from Wolverton to Newport Pagnell on Friday, 3 August 1962. A casual and happy four-mile branch line, the passengers and locals affectionately knew the train as 'Newport Nobby'. *(E. A. Cook)*

Opposite top: 8. On the opposite side of the main line was the entrance to the Newport Pagnell branch, which had a connecting spur to the 'up' slow, forming a triangle. The works used this facility for turning the Royal Train coaches. 'Newport Nobby' (alias Webb 0-6-2 coal tank No. 7763) squeals round the curve heading for Bradwell on 26 March 1931. *(W. J. S. Meredith)*

9. An example of a third class ticket from Bradwell to Wolverton dated 20 October 1928.

Opposite bottom: 10. Wolverton carriage works possessed some veteran ex-L.N.W.R. Ramsbottom/ Webb 0-6-0 saddle tanks for shunting purposes. Constructed between 1870 and 1880, the last was not withdrawn until 1959. Here we see CARRIAGE DEPARTMENT No. 3 shunting the yard on 18 October 1955. *(F. W. Shuttleworth)*

Opposite 11. Sudden activity at Newport Pagnell, as the 1.00 p.m. departure time arrives for No. 41222 to propel its push-and-pull set away towards Wolverton on Wednesday, 30 August 1961. Up until the mid-1950s the engine stayed on the branch permanently, having its own small wooden shed at Newport Pagnell. (*E. A. Cook*)

Above: 12. What a superbly rural scene at Bradwell on 27 March 1931! Webb Coal tank No. 7763 takes on water during its short stop *en route* to Newport Pagnell. The water came from the same main that supplied the houses in the village, and pressure dropped alarmingly when 'Newport Nobby' was filling its tanks. After complaints from housewives, the use of the water column was banned on a Monday (washing day) and then totally as Bradwell grew in size; water then had to be obtained from the low pressure column at Wolverton. (*W. J. S. Meredith*)

13. Stanier 2-6-4 tank No. 42454 idles away the hours on an engineering train south of Wolverton station in May 1962. In the background work proceeds on alterations to the road bridge, no doubt in preparation for the forthcoming electrification. A few ripples disturb the reflections on the surface of the Grand Union Canal. *(W. J. S. Meredith)*

Above: 14. A peaceful scene at Castlethorpe station around the time of the First World War. In the station on the up slow, a Webb Jubilee class, 4 cylinder compound 4-4-0 stands at the head of a local stopping train. *(Northamptonshire Libraries)*

Right: 15. Bowen-Cooke George the Fifth No. 882 CANADA pilots a Claughton 4-6-0 over Castlethorpe water troughs on this very fast stretch of line, with the up 'Irish Mail' during 6 August 1927. The seventeen vehicles are painted in L.M.S. livery, but CANADA still retains her L.N.W.R. livery and number, over four years after the L.M.S. was formed. When trains are double-headed, only one locomotive can pick up water at a time, in this instance CANADA. *(L. J. Thompson)*

Above: 16. Ashton, 12 April 1962, finds Princess Royal Pacific No. 46209 PRINCESS BEATRICE roaring past a down freight, heading for Euston with her express from Blackpool. This was the period when the Princess Royals were returned to service, having previously been put into store. *(K. Fairey)*

Opposite: 17. An abundance of power here as Royal Scots No. 46148 THE MANCHESTER REGIMENT and No. 46140 THE KING'S ROYAL RIFLE CORPS cruise past Ashton with a down express on 16 June 1951. No. 46140 was rebuilt with a taper boiler the following May, while No. 46148 survived until July 1954 before being treated likewise. *(L. Hanson)*

18. Two lone passengers stand on platform 2 at Roade station, as Royal Scot class No. 46129 THE SCOTTISH HORSE sweeps past with a northbound express on Monday, 7 August 1961, leaving a trail of smoke to linger amongst the station buildings. Trainspotting from the platforms was discouraged due to the high speeds the steam-hauled expresses came past. However, the sensation of standing near to one of these trains as they sped past was too good to miss and an experience never to be forgotten, even if it meant being chased off by the stationmaster! (L. W. Roy)

THE PREMIER LINE

19. Carlisle-based Black 5 No. 45323 slowly brings a Bank Holiday relief train into platform 3 at Roade station on 7 August 1961. Roade station was the first stop on a Northampton to Euston train, and many trainspotters used to travel from Northampton to stay at the station all day. The chance to see both main and slow line trains was one of the main attractions. The station sadly closed on 7 September 1964. *(L. W. Roy)*

20. Having swept through Roade cutting, the driver of the 12.25 p.m. express from Blackpool Central to Euston, shuts off steam on Stanier Jubilee No. 45571 SOUTH AFRICA as he sees a distant signal south of Roade station set at danger. Hold ups were not unusual, with all the extra traffic at holiday periods, as on this Bank Holiday Monday, 7 August 1961. (L. W. Roy)

21. What a tranquil scene at Roade station on Bank Holiday Monday, 7 August 1961! In the warm sunshine trainspotters are well in evidence, positioned in their usual places on the bank and fences, while a relief Rugby to Euston train waits to leave platform 4 behind Black 5 No. 44771. The first sign of things to come appears on the main line in the shape of a diesel-hauled express to London. Even today, although alas the station has gone, the background scene is still very much the same, dominated by *The George* public house opposite the old station master's house and station booking hall. (*L. W. Roy*)

Left: 22. The photographer nearly always carried a camera with him and Sunday, 30 May 1937 was no exception. A stop at Black Bridge to see if anything was about found 'Baby Scot' (Patriot class) No. 5504 ROYAL SIGNALS hurrying up from Blisworth towards Roade cutting with her rake of maroon coaches. The line to Northampton curves away under the bridge on the right. (*L. Hanson*)

Right: 23. Only loaded to seven bogies, it's a mere bagatelle for Royal Scot No. 6140 HECTOR racing through Roade cutting with a Euston-bound express in the mid-1930s. Smoke from trains made conditions inside the 'signal box on stilts' over the Northampton line somewhat uncomfortable at times, especially when a train was working hard up the gradient from the town. Even with the windows and door shut, the smoke penetrated inside and lingered for sometime. The signal box only controlled the adjacent signals and, being a usual twenty-four hour a day box, it required three men on shifts to work it, access being gained by walking down the track from Roade station or across the fields and down the bank. Not surprisingly, this was considered uneconomic by the L.M.S. who installed intermediate block colour lights, thus making the signal box redundant. Demolition took place during the Second World War circa 1940. (*W. J. S. Meredith*)

24. Entering Roade cutting, Stanier Coronation Pacific No. 46234 DUCHESS OF ABERCORN works back into her stride after the Blisworth stop, hauling the ex-8.30 a.m. Carlisle to Euston express during 1959. The first vehicle behind the tender is a Gresley full brake parcels van. (*L. W. Roy*)

25. Ex-works crimson lake Royal Scot No. 6105 CAMERON HIGH-LANDER enters the north end of Blisworth station at very high speed. She is heavily loaded with sixteen coaches, hauling the Saturdays only Cockermouth to Euston express at 2.34 p.m. on 13 August 1932. (*L. Hanson*)

Boyhood Memories at Blisworth

Sitting in the Railway Station
Waiting for the next Express,
Spotter's notebook at the ready
Well thumbed, greasy, such a mess.

A bell sounds in the signal box,
Levers pulled and wires thread,
Home and distant signals rising
Show the road is clear ahead.

Gosh! it seems an age while waiting
Till I hear that muffled roar,
Not much more anticipating
Very soon I'll know the score.

Round the curve, here comes the engine
Very fast, her pistons purr,
Drawing closer to the station
Whistle screaming, rods a blur.

All things seem to be vibrating
Smoke and steam swirl in the sky,
How my heart is palpitating,
A speck of ash gets in my eye.

46231 the number,
'Duchess of Atholl' is the name,
Fourteen coaches behind her tender
Announcing proudly 'The Royal Scot' train.

On they clatter through the station
Passengers blind to spotters' looks,
Rushing to their destinations
As slipstream tugs at clothes and books.

Off they go into the distance
Bucking and swaying down the track,
Home and distant return to danger,
All of a sudden, peace is back.

Do girls bring as much excitement?
In a different way no doubt,
A few more years will give the answer
When love is in and trains are out.

Footsteps shake me from my daydream
Echoing in the subway clear;
The Porter bellows down the platform
'Come on now lad, you can't stop 'ere.'

26. Poem by Richard Coleman.

27. The driver of Stanier Jubilee No. 45601 BRITISH GUIANA gives the photographer in Blisworth signal box a wry smile, as he awaits the 'right away' with his Euston to Birmingham excursion on Sunday, 6 July 1952. The train normally travelled via Northampton, but on this day was kept to the main line by engineering works on the loop. A connecting service would be put on from the town to Blisworth. (Ross Smith)

28. Orange reflections from the setting sun on Fowler Patriot No. 45538 GIGGLESWICK create a dramatic scene at Blisworth late one afternoon in November 1959. Even the fireman has time to relax and admire it all. The Patriots thrived on the old L.N.W.R. method of heavy firing, in complete contrast to their Jubilee counterparts, which required the little and often technique. (See illustration 31). *(Tony Heighton)*

THE PREMIER LINE

29. Stanier Black 5 No. 45272 hurries the afternoon Camden to Carlisle express freight (known as the 'Doodlebug') through the bleak winter landscape north of Blisworth station on Thursday, 17 January 1963. The fireman observes the jets of steam blowing from a leaking steam chest cock, but it will not noticeably affect the train's progress. *(K. Fairey)*

Opposite: 30. A very smart signalman Parry stands inside Gayton signal box on a summer's day in 1947, rightly proud of its spotless condition. Many is the time he will have received the series of bell codes from the next signal box, one ring to call him up, then four in quick succession, indicating an express passenger was due.

In swinging over the levers to pull off the semaphore signals, he will often have heard the cry from trainspotters in the field opposite 'peg on the main', resulting in fellow enthusiasts making a mad rush to the fence, ready for a closer look at the oncoming engine.

After a short wait the bell would ring out twice more as the train entered the section of track controlled by Gayton signal box, followed quickly by the express as up to five hundred tons of locomotive and coaches thundered and clattered by.

A glance across the tracks at the trainspotters' faces would tell signalman Parry if the locomotive had been a rare visitor or just one of the regulars. *(R. J. Rawlinson)*

Above: 31. Fowler Patriot 4-6-0 No. 45538 GIGGLESWICK hurries southwards with a fast fitted freight past Gayton Loops, as daylight fades on a very pleasant November day in 1959. What a great pity that no member of this class survived into preservation. (See illustration 28). *(Tony Heighton)*

THE PREMIER LINE   BLETCHLEY TO RUGBY

Above: 32. Viewed from the signal box at the busy Banbury Lane crossing at 8.45 a.m. on 3 August 1957, a Stanier Black 5 works southwards with its 6.40 a.m. ex-Wolverhampton to Euston train. With the signal box limited to working crossing gates and signals, one signalman spent his entire career here without ever changing a point. *(P.I. Rawlinson)*

Opposite: 33. The Euston to Manchester down 'Comet' slams past Banbury Lane signal box at 11.00 a.m. on a February morning in 1953, with two month old Britannia Pacific No. 70034 THOMAS HARDY in charge. Situated on the Banbury lane, between Rothersthorpe and Pattishall villages, the signal box was always regularly visited by local enthusiasts. To stand by the crossing gates or inside the box and watch the trains thrash past was an exhilarating experience on every occasion. It was therefore a sad loss when the signal box was finally closed and dismantled in 1988. *(R. Gammage)*

THE PREMIER LINE   BLETCHLEY TO RUGBY

Left opposite: 34/35. On 21 September 1951 the 8.20 a.m. Liverpool to Euston train was travelling south of Weedon at about sixty m.p.h., when the leading bogey of Princess Royal Pacific No. 46207 PRINCESS ARTHUR OF CONNAUGHT became derailed, plunging the locomotive down the bank and wrecking the train. The coaches were cleared and the line opened to traffic within two days, but the locomotive lay forlornly on its side for over a month while the Motive Power Department decided on the best method of recovery. A temporary ramp was excavated, and track laid down to the locomotive. Finally on 28 October 1951, and after much preparation, two cranes and five Stanier 8F 2-8-0s positioned themselves to either lift, pull or stabilise the loco during the recovery operation. In these photographs the moment of truth has arrived, as anxious officials watch PRINCESS ARTHUR OF CONNAUGHT being hauled successfully back onto its wheels. A defective front bogey on No. 46207 caused the accident, and sadly fifteen people lost their lives. *(R. Gammage)*

Below: 36. This rare photograph taken from the steps of Heyford signal box shows Jubilee class No. 45625 Sᴀʀᴀᴡᴀᴋ accelerating towards London with the 6.15 a.m. (Sunday) express from Heysham to Euston on 11 July 1954. In the background can be seen the 492 yards long Stowe Hill tunnel, while 8F class No. 48008 waits in the loop for a gap in the traffic. *(Ross Smith)*

Opposite top: 37. Signalman Frank Denny 'takes a breather' at Heyford signal box on Tuesday, 18 July 1950. When he retired in 1957 he had completed fifty years service with the railway, working on the L.N.W.R., L.M.S. and B.R. *(Ross Smith)*

Above: 38. In the bay platform at Weedon station, the driver watches his fireman preparing to fill the water tanks of Ivatt 2-6-2 tank No. 41227. A very sunny and pleasant day in September 1958, just ideal for relaxing on this branch line train to Warwick. *(P. I. Rawlinson)*

39. A wet Braunston station during the winter of 1959. The staff is about to be handed to the fireman of the Stanier 8F, so that the train can proceed on its journey towards Weedon, hauling its load of chalk empties. These chalk trains originated from Leighton Buzzard and were left in the sidings at Blisworth. From Blisworth a Northampton engine took over the train, and continued via Weedon to the cement works at Southam. A maximum of fifty wagons was allowed on the branch. A train of empties would then be taken back to Blisworth, where the number of wagons could be increased to seventy for the remaining journey to Leighton Buzzard. *(Tony Heighton)*

THE PREMIER LINE

40. Ivatt 2-6-2 tank No. 41214 of Rugby shed pauses at Braunston station with its solitary coach on Saturday, 4 September 1954. The train is the 9.00 a.m. local from Weedon to Warwick, and the coach on this occasion is brake 3rd No. M6000. *(Ian L. Wright)*

41. The classic view of the southern approach to Rugby Midland station, unusual in that it is seen from a moving train. Patriot class No. 5535 SIR HERBERT WALKER K.C.B. at the front of a Euston to Birmingham train, comes off the Northampton line on Sunday, 11 December 1938 and coasts past the famous L.N.W.R. signal gantry. The gantry was erected and maintained at the expense of the Great Central as part of the way-leave agreement when their viaduct, built in 1897, would have made a confused background to the existing signals. To avoid this the whole gantry was duplicated, with an upper set of signal arms which were seen against a sky background. Fabricated at Crewe in 1896, it had forty-four arms on twenty-six posts. Controlling it and the associated junctions took 15,000 lever movements every twenty-four hours from Rugby No. 1 signal box. It was finally dismantled in 1939 after electric colour lights were installed. Also of note is the chequered board under the bridge abutment, indicating the location of a travelling post office lineside apparatus for the exchange of mail.
(W. J. S. Meredith)

42. Sunday, 28 October 1934 finds an interesting front-end line up of ex-L.N.W.R. and L.M.S. locomotives outside Rugby shed. Nearest the camera are three Rugby-based engines in the form of Webb Cauliflower 2F 0-6-0 No. 8597, Bowen-Cooke Prince of Wales 4-6-0 No. 25602 Bonaventure, and Whale Precursor 4-4-0 No. 5303 Argus. Behind these a visiting Fowler 'Baby Scot' 4-6-0 brews up ready for departure later in the afternoon. A member of the ex-L.N.W.R. G1 class 0-8-0, later known as 'Super Ds', comes next and finally the tender end of a modern Stanier locomotive. These represent five different designers and fifty-four years of development. (*W. J. S. Meredith*)

THE PREMIER LINE: BLETCHLEY TO RUGBY

43. June 1919 finds a straw boatered enthusiast observing L.N.W.R. Whale Experiment class 4-6-0 No. 353 BRITANNIC receiving attention from her crew, as she patiently awaits departure time at the head of an up local at the south end of Rugby station. This particular locomotive was fitted with experimental bogey shields. *(L. J. Thompson)*

Above: 44. In contrast to the L.N.W.R. locomotive opposite, a Midland Compound 4-4-0 No. 41174 eases out from Rugby station into the sunlight, hauling her rake of red and cream coaches on Saturday, 8 March 1952, working the 4.33 p.m. stopping train to Leicester. *(Ross Smith)*

Right: 45. Pre-gummed luggage labels were printed for the passenger's use, various examples of which appear throughout these pages (illustrations 69, 83, 93, 158). *(Tony Heighton)*

L. & N. W. RY.
Rugby

Above: 47. Early morning on Sunday, 10 October 1954 finds Stanier Coronation Pacific No. 46226 DUCHESS OF NORFOLK drifting into the north end of Rugby station. Proudly carrying the four headlamp code and with her paintwork burnished to perfection, she heads the Royal Train conveying Her Majesty the Queen between Ballater and Euston. (*Derek Smith*)

Opposite: 46. Having drawn into Rugby Midland station with a very long passenger and parcels train on Tuesday, 4 April 1961, the crew of Fowler Patriot No. 45549 requested assistance for the remainder of the journey southwards. Rugby Black 5 No. 44831 duly obliged, and linked on to the front of the Patriot as pilot engine. The crew exchange details on this dismal wet day, before departing from under one of Rugby's colour light signals. (*K. Fairey*)

THE PREMIER LINE: BLETCHLEY TO RUGBY

48. The station clock on platform 1 at Rugby Midland station shows 5.10 p.m., and there is a bustle of activity as Patriot class No. 45536 PRIVATE W. WOOD V.C. stands at the head of the 3.50 p.m. Euston to Manchester express on Thursday, 11 June 1959. With some fifteen minutes to departure time, there is still plenty of time for the driver to check over his engine while the station vendor endeavours to sell the contents of his trolley. Rugby-based Black 5 No. 44863 impatiently waits in the shadows of the express for its next duty. (Tony Heighton)

THE PREMIER LINE

49. Rugby Midland station on Thursday, 11 June 1959 and the 5.35 p.m. train to Leamington waits in bay platform 6 with Warwick-based Ivatt tank No. 41227 in charge. Over enthusiastic watering causes the fireman to knock off the water supply by kicking the lever, so as not to get soaked as the water cascades dramatically off the side of the locomotive. Two days later, on Saturday, 13 June, 41227 was to have the dubious honour of hauling the last passenger train to Leamington – the 7.54 p.m. from Rugby, ending 108 years of passenger traffic on the line. *(Tony Heighton)*

GREAT CENTRAL METALS RUGBY TO BRACKLEY

50. A classic example of an Annesley 'runner' on the Great Central. Annesley 9F No. 92093 hurries its Annesley to Woodford freight through the 'birdcage' passing over the West Coast main line at Rugby on Saturday, 20 June 1959. This freight service was to prove to be the most outstanding feature of the line in its last years. It was incomparable and became a show piece of efficiency. The trains were called 'runners' or 'windcutters' by the railwaymen, and for nine years (1957–66) the 9Fs were an essential part of the Great Central scene, speeding these non-stop freights between Nottingham and Woodford. The magnificent girder bridge still remains intact to this day – a memory to a once great main line. (*R. A. F. Puryer*)

51. The 'Master Cutler' was the principal express on the Great Central. It was introduced in October 1947 and ran from Sheffield to Marylebone. Its final stop before the London terminus was Rugby Central, and in this view one of Leicester Central shed's best and favourite A3 locomotives No. 60107 ROYAL LANCER rushes into the station on a freezing sunny morning in February 1955, before its 9.46 a.m. departure time. Alas, by the start of 1958 the 'Master Cutler' train had been transferred to the Great Northern line, and the Great Central version ran for only a further two years. (J. Harrison)

Right: 52. It is Cup Final day at Wembley and Leicester City meet the Spurs on Saturday, 6 May 1961. Shed staff at Leicester Central make sure that local pride isn't neglected by cleaning all the locomotives used on the special trains. The shed's only serviceable V2 No. 60890 is at the head of one of the 'First Class only' trains as it storms out of Catesby tunnel at the summit of the six mile climb from Braunston. Although Leicester were to lose on this occasion, they were to return to Wembley two years later. *(L. W. Roy)*

Below: 53. Sheffield B1 class No. 61044 steams freely out of Catesby tunnel with a Nottingham to Marylebone 'semi-fast' on the same day. Catesby tunnel was one and three quarter miles long and was built through the Northamptonshire clay. Its lining required some thirty million bricks in up to six layers! *(L. W. Roy)*

Above: 54. York-based V2 class No. 60828 in charge of the 5.10 a.m. York to Cardiff goods, clatters through Rugby Central with its three-cylinder staccato beat echoing around the station signal box, on a bitterly cold winter's day on Saturday, 27 February 1965. This freight train was normally called 'The Welshman', and was worked by a York locomotive as far as Woodford. There the train would have a fairly long stop before continuing south behind a W.R. Hall class locomotive to Cardiff. *(Derek Smith)*

55. Neasden Standard class 5 No. 73045 heads north through Charwelton station on Saturday, 6 May 1961 with the 12.25 p.m. semi-fast from Marylebone to Nottingham Victoria. At this time on the Great Central this train was one of only three semi-fast trains that ran each way between the two cities. They were mainly six coach formations without refreshment facilities! The station itself finally closed on 4 March 1963. (L. W. Roy)

GREAT CENTRAL METALS

Above: 56. The Woodford to Rugby local train makes a spirited departure from Charwelton station behind Woodford engine L1 class No. 67789 on Thursday, 22 March 1962. Mineral wagons both sides of the station show that ironstone traffic was still flourishing. The nearby Charwelton and Byfield quarries possessed the only rail worked pits in the area, and Charwelton was the only ironstone system that connected with the Great Central line. *(K. Fairey)*

Right: 57. An example of one of the Great Central station lamps at Charwelton station in 1958.
(Tony Heighton)

RUGBY TO BRACKLEY

59. A summer Saturday on the Great Central, and the holiday season is in full swing. Among the many holiday trains Hall class No. 6979 HELPERLY HALL from Banbury shed, bustles the Bournemouth to Newcastle train through Woodford yard and past the carriage and wagon repair depot on 15 July 1961. On these inter-regional trains the Banbury engine and crew worked to Leicester and then returned on another southbound train. On the right stands Woodford No. 2 signal box, one of the four boxes that controlled the extensive yards and connections at Woodford. *(R. A. F. Puryer)*

Opposite: 58. A Saturday afternoon look inside Woodford Halse locomotive shed finds York V2 class No. 60982 taking a long rest on 11 April 1964, before it would be required to return north with a Woodford to York goods train. *(George Smith)*

GREAT CENTRAL METALS
RUGBY TO BRACKLEY

60. Just south of Woodford Halse the Stratford-upon-Avon and Midland Junction Railway crossed over the Great Central. On Saturday, 15 July 1961 Stanier 8F No. 48290 ambles along, tender first, with her Blisworth to Woodford West branch freight, and is about to rumble over the bridge spanning the Great Central tracks below. The bridge, built wide enough to allow for extension of the double tracks at Woodford West Junction, was never fully utilised. (*R.A.F.Puryer*)

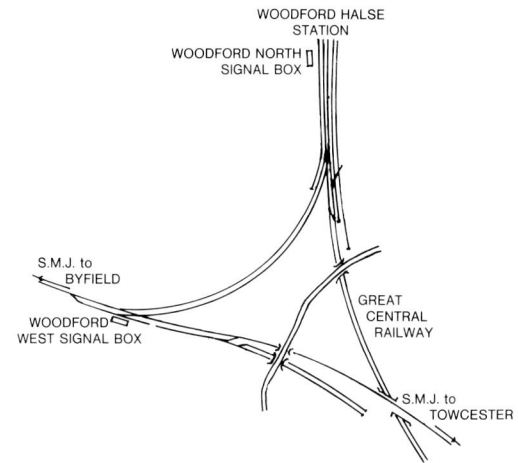

WOODFORD HALSE STATION

WOODFORD NORTH SIGNAL BOX

S.M.J. to BYFIELD

WOODFORD WEST SIGNAL BOX

GREAT CENTRAL RAILWAY

S.M.J. to TOWCESTER

61. Having picked up her freight from Woodford Halse, Hall 4-6-0 No. 6952 KIMBERLEY HALL gets to grips with her load as she strides purposefully round the spur to join up with the S.M.J. at Woodford West Junction during September 1961, bound for Cardiff. The train probably originated at York, and would have been hauled by 'V2' as far as Woodford. It would then travel via the S.M.J. to Cardiff, thus cutting out the bottleneck at Birmingham. (Dr. G. C. Farnell)

62. Station staff pose for the camera by the impressive nameboard at the south end of Woodford station during the days of the Great Central. It is interesting to note the gas lamps fixed to the top of the nameboard, a tradition perpetuated to the end at Brackley Central (see illustration 65). *(Courtesy H. Blencowe)*

Above: 63. On Thursday, 9 March 1899, three special trains ran from Manchester, Sheffield and Nottingham, transporting guests to Marylebone for the opening ceremony of the London extension to the Great Central Railway. In this picture, the excitement mounts as Pollitt class 11A 4-4-0 No. 270, adorned with flags, runs into Brackley Central *en route* to Marylebone. *(L. Varney N.R.O. ref YZ 4191)*

Right: 64. White-bearded Squire Stratton of Turweston appears not to share the excitement of the occasion, while one assumes the firemen next to him are in attendance just in case of some unforeseen eventuality. *(L. Varney N.R.O. ref YZ 4191)*

Opposite: 65. A superb view of a typical Great Central station – Brackley Central on a hot summer's day in 1959. Every part of the station is neat and tidy with flower beds decorating the platform. Leicester's V2 class engine No. 60879 arrives with the 8.30 a.m. Manchester to Marylebone train, as passengers gather on the platform and the porter awaits his next duty. Alas by 5 September 1966 the station had closed to passenger traffic.
(Betty Hutchings A.R.P.S.)

Above: 66. A rare passenger duty for a York-based 'Bloodspitter' or more officially known as ex-L.N.E.R. B16/2 class 4-6-0 No. 61455, waiting to depart from Brackley Central Station with a semi-fast train from Marylebone to Nottingham on Monday 24 July 1961.

At this time if a N.E. engine appeared in Annesley yard it was common practice for it to be used by engine crews, who had a preference for Eastern Region locomotives, on a 'stolen trip' to Marylebone and back on one of the semi-fasts, before the engine was sent home. *(Keith Adams)*

MIDLAND MAIN LINE

67. St. Pancras station 1958, and what a glorious scene to greet the Midland line traveller as he waits to catch his train to the Midlands! Swirling steam and smoke rise to the arched roof, while whistles and rhythmic exhausts of the departing trains echo around this great London terminus, creating the unique characteristics of a steam worked railway. *(Tony Heighton)*

ST PANCRAS: BEDFORD TO MARKET HARBOROUGH AND HARRINGWORTH

Above: 68. The largest single span station roof in Great Britain, built by the Midland Railway in 1868, towers over the platforms at St. Pancras station, and presents a magnificent spectacle under which Royal Scot class No. 46132 THE KING'S REGIMENT LIVERPOOL is waiting to depart with the 4.10 p.m. express to Sheffield in 1961. Within an hour the train will be steaming through the twenty miles of Northamptonshire countryside, calling at Wellingborough and Kettering stations. No doubt many local travellers will recall this classic view from the steam age. *(L. W. Roy)*

69. Luggage label.

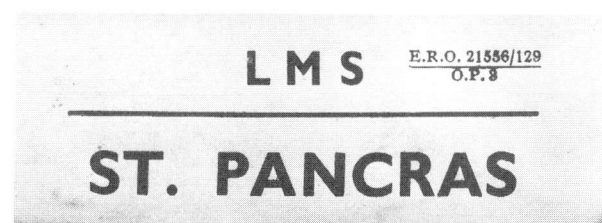

LMS   E.R.O. 21556/129
                    O.P. 3

ST. PANCRAS

70. Bedford shed yard in the summer of 1956. This view under the Ford End Road bridge shows class 4F No. 44043 standing at the head of the 'legs' road, while ex-L. & Y.R. tank No. 50646 stands in the 'new' road, the latter having been transferred to the Bedford area for a short period at this time. *(P. Martin)*

71. At Ouse Bridge, Bedford, on the up line to Hitchin, Stanier Black 5 No. 44985 eases its way back towards a track maintenance gang with its load of ballast on Thursday, 28 March 1963. The Midland main line passes under Ford End Road bridge in the background and into the Midland Road station behind. This superb view of 'top end' yard was taken from the footbridge adjacent to the River Ouse, and shows a classic example of a typical railway yard in steam days. (K. Fairey)

72. Classic view of a 'Jubilee' on the Midland main line! No. 45561 SASKATCHEWAN waits for the road at Bedford Midland Road station with the 4.26 p.m. to St. Pancras express during the summer of 1959, with the Ford End Road bridge framing the scene. The 'Jubilees' epitomised haulage of the passenger services on the Midland main line from the late 1930s onwards, and achieved a high reputation amongst railwaymen and enthusiasts alike. (L. W. Roy)

73. With their six feet nine inch driving wheels and taper boiler, the Stanier Jubilees gave the impression of being real racing machines, and in the right hands very often were. They gave their best when they were fired little and often, and worked on full regulator with short cut offs.

Well burnished and superbly lit, Jubilee No. 45636 UGANDA waits patiently for clearance from Bedford North's main station starter signal at Bedford Midland Road station, on a glorious summer's evening in 1961. The young lad gazes in admiration, longing to be asked up onto the footplate. (L. W. Roy)

74. Wellingborough 9F No. 92056 hoists a canopy of smoke into the still November sky, as it toils up the bank past Irchester North signal box with a heavy coal train from Wellingborough to Brent yard in London in 1959. A fine study of a locomotive class that represented the climax of British steam engine development. (Tony Heighton)

MIDLAND MAIN LINE
BEDFORD TO MARKET HARBOROUGH
AND HARRINGWORTH

75. Held up by a signal check, Stanier Jubilee No. 45561 SAS-KATCHEWAN powers up the gradient past Souldrop signal box, endeavouring to make up lost time hauling her Sheffield-bound express on 21 April 1960. The signalman's more mundane means of transport stands on the opposite side of the tracks, awaiting the end of his shift. (K. Fairey)

76. Shadows lengthen as the late afternoon sunshine falls on this November 1959 view at Irchester station. 4F class No. 44156, a Wellingborough locomotive, drags a pick-up goods train along the slow line towards Sharnbrook tunnel. The station building, which can be partially seen on the right, was unique in that it was built astride the running lines on the road overbridge unlike any other intermediate station. Passenger traffic at the station ended on 7 March 1960 but goods traffic continued until 4 January 1965. *(Tony Heighton)*

MIDLAND MAIN LINE
BEDFORD TO MARKET HARBOROUGH AND HARRINGWORTH

77. A fine example of a gas lamp and station totem sign at Irchester station in 1959. *(Tony Heighton)*

78. Having just entered Northamptonshire near Irchester South signal box, 01 class No. 63725 drifts quickly down the gradient towards Irchester station with an empty wagon train in July 1956. An unusual class of locomotive to be seen in the area, No. 63725 came to Wellingborough during July 1956. It stayed some five months, during which time it was used on trials, on the Midland main line on various train duties, before being transferred to Annesley shed in December 1956. *(J. Harrison)*

79. A Beyer-Garratt class locomotive No. 47994 in appalling external condition brings a train of iron ore past Wellingborough Midland Road station on Thursday, 3 October 1957. The iron ore is from Irchester quarries, and is bound for the steelworks on Teesside. Scurrying backwards, light engine, towards the station is class 3F No. 43624. No. 47994 had the honour of being the last of the thirty-three Beyer-Garratts to remain in service, and was withdrawn the following year after twenty-eight years of service. *(K. Fairey)*

Above: 80. Easter Monday 1959, and the rain-soaked platforms at Wellingborough Midland Road station bear witness to yet another express, as Trafford Park Britannia No. 70015 APOLLO sweeps past a solitary schoolboy admirer with a Manchester train. *(D.F.J. Rowe)*

Right: 81. Busy north end of Wellingborough station on a hot sunny Thursday, 24 July 1958. Immaculately clean Trafford Park Britannia class No. 70004 WILLIAM SHAKESPEARE hurtles through with the 4.25 p.m. St. Pancras to Manchester Central express, passing 9F class No. 92160 in charge of a Brent to Wellingborough empty coal train. No. 70004 was probably the most distinguished of all the 'Britannias'. During its stay on the Southern Region the engine was allocated to work the famous *Golden Arrow* boat train, and was always maintained in superb condition. On its transfer to the London Midland Region it obviously hadn't lost its sparkle! *(K. Fairey)*

Above: 82. Fowler 4F class No. 44243 from Kentish Town heads a mixed freight train past Wellingborough station signal box on the slow line to London in June 1959. The unglamorous nature of the freight train is well in evidence, as only the young trainspotter is bothered to look round amongst the group of passengers waiting for their train on platform 2. *(P. I. Rawlinson)*

83. Luggage label.

P. F. 70.

R 2.

Midland Railway.

WELLINGBORO'

84. Both driver and fireman pose for the photograph as Royal Scot class No. 46122 ROYAL ULSTER RIFLEMAN, shedded at Trafford Park, restarts a Manchester-bound express at Wellingborough Midland Road station during the late summer of 1961. In the background is the large hostel or lodging house for railwaymen, conveniently built adjacent to the locomotive sheds. One wonders how much sleep was obtained with the noise of the railway at work continuing throughout the night! (L. W. Roy)

85. 'Jinty' class No. 7554 potters about, shunting 'Tipperary' sidings opposite Wellingborough No. 2 shed during the summer of 1947. In the background one of the Beyer-Garratt locomotives is parked in between duties. The main function of the shed was to provide freight engines for the Midland main lines to move the vast amount of freight traffic, especially coal and iron ore. (R. J. Rawlinson)

MIDLAND MAIN LINE

Left: 86. Crab class No. 42823 gathers speed as it climbs past Wellingborough No. 2 shed with the afternoon Burton empties, amid the lengthening shadows of the day during 1958. The winter sunshine reflects dramatically off the side of the train, creating a superb glint effect. *(J. Harrison)*

BEDFORD TO MARKET HARBOROUGH AND HARRINGWORTH

Right: 87. Royal Scot class No. 46133 THE GREEN HOWARDS drifts past Wellingborough North signal box and a shed full of locomotives with an express for St. Pancras on Saturday, 13 June 1959. The external condition of the signal box suggests it was not the most pleasant of places to work. In fact it was very difficult to keep smoke from locomotives out of the box, and at times if locomen didn't get along with the duty signalman, locomotives would be purposely left directly outside the box, and smoke drifting in would make life unbearable, especially on hot summer days. *(R. Hodgkins)*

88. A Sunday view inside the roundhouse of Wellingborough No. 2 shed during July 1956 shows a line up of Wellingborough locomotives; from left to right Nos. 48625, 47543, 41277, 47273 and 48614 all at rest, awaiting their next turn of duty. This particular ex-Midland Railway 'square' roundhouse was built in 1872, and accommodated steam locomotives until 1966. In the late 1960s the shed was taken over by Whitworths Holdings Ltd., and hence gained a new lease of life. This was surely a tribute to the outstanding Midland design, and even today the shed continues to be used. (P. I. Rawlinson)

89. Opposite the shed yard at Wellingborough on 27 May 1930, a well cleaned Johnson 2P No. 541 prepares to shunt the stock of its local passenger train. In the shed yard Fowler 4F No. 4157 and Johnson 2F No. 3121 still retain the first style of L.M.S. goods livery, with L.M.S. in small letters on the cabside and the number in large numerals on the tender. This caused confusion, as tenders were split from locomotives during overhaul and not always matched up again. Consequently engines were seen running with one number on the smokebox door and a different one on the tender. Hence the reason for placing the number on the cabside as on No. 541. *(L. Hanson)*

MIDLAND MAIN LINE
BEDFORD TO MARKET HARBOROUGH AND HARRINGWORTH

Opposite: 90. A view of the north end of Wellingborough locomotive shed area and yard, as seen from Finedon Road bridge. Beyer-Garratt No. 47980 works past Wellingborough 'Down' sidings on the 'reception' road with a Wellingborough (London Road) to Teeside (Cargo Fleet) iron ore train during the summer of 1956. This class of freight locomotive was part of the everyday scene at Wellingborough, from their introduction in 1930 until their withdrawal in the mid-50s. With their 45,620 lb. tractive effort they were regularly found on Toton–Brent coal trains amongst their many other freight duties. *(R. Gammage)*

Above: 91. Standard class 5 No. 73142 strides past the site of the former Finedon station, which closed to passenger traffic as early as December 1940, with a fitted goods train to Rowsley yard on Thursday, 3 May 1962 as lineside workers take their lunch break. The Midland Railway designed signal, station architecture and the signal box are still very much in evidence at this time. *(K. Fairey)*

Above: 92. Station Road approach to Kettering station in July 1964. The marvellous collection of cars of the period as well as the goods yard, the signal box, semaphore signalling and Midland Railway station building, which dates from 1857, all help to give the feel of the local railway scene as it was in the late '50s and early '60s. *(W. J. S. Meredith)*

93. Luggage label.

Midland Railway. P. F. 70.

R 2a

KETTERING

MIDLAND MAIN LINE

94. The later years of steam on the Midland line saw the use of many rebuilt 'Royal Scots' on expresses. This illustration shows a fine study of Royal Scot class No. 46123 ROYAL IRISH FUSILIER as it stands in platform 4 in the evening light at Kettering station, with a train from Sheffield to London in the summer of 1961. By October 1962 the locomotive was withdrawn. (L. W. Roy)

BEDFORD TO MARKET HARBOROUGH
AND HARRINGWORTH

95. This excellently composed picture, taken from the north end of
Kettering station on Thursday, 18 January 1962, shows 9F class
No. 92104 drifting down the gradient with a southbound coal train.
In the background Kettering North signal box, together with its
marvellous collection of signals, are prominent, as is the chimney
to the right of the locomotive showing the site of the Kettering gas
works. (K. Fairey)

MIDLAND MAIN LINE
BEDFORD TO MARKET HARBOROUGH
AND HARRINGWORTH

96. Activity at Kettering locomotive shed in September 1964. A couple of 8F class locomotives No. 48177 and No. 48530 prepare to leave the yard now that the early morning commuter traffic has passed. A car park in Northfield Avenue adjacent to the shed yard shows the wide variety of the 50s and 60s road transport available at this time, all in excellent external condition, unlike the steam locomotives. *(W. J. S. Meredith)*

97. Kettering driver Fred Betts oils his engine class 8F No. 48381 in February 1962. One of the old traditional railwaymen, complete with polished shoes, he spent a lifetime on the railway and retired when the steam era finished in 1965. *(M. Winnett)*

98. Kettering engine cleaner Mike Winnett takes a break from his duties to pose for a photograph on class 3F No. 43249 at Kettering loco-shed during 1959. He later became a fireman before the steam ended, and continued his career on the railways as a driver. *(M. Winnett collection)*

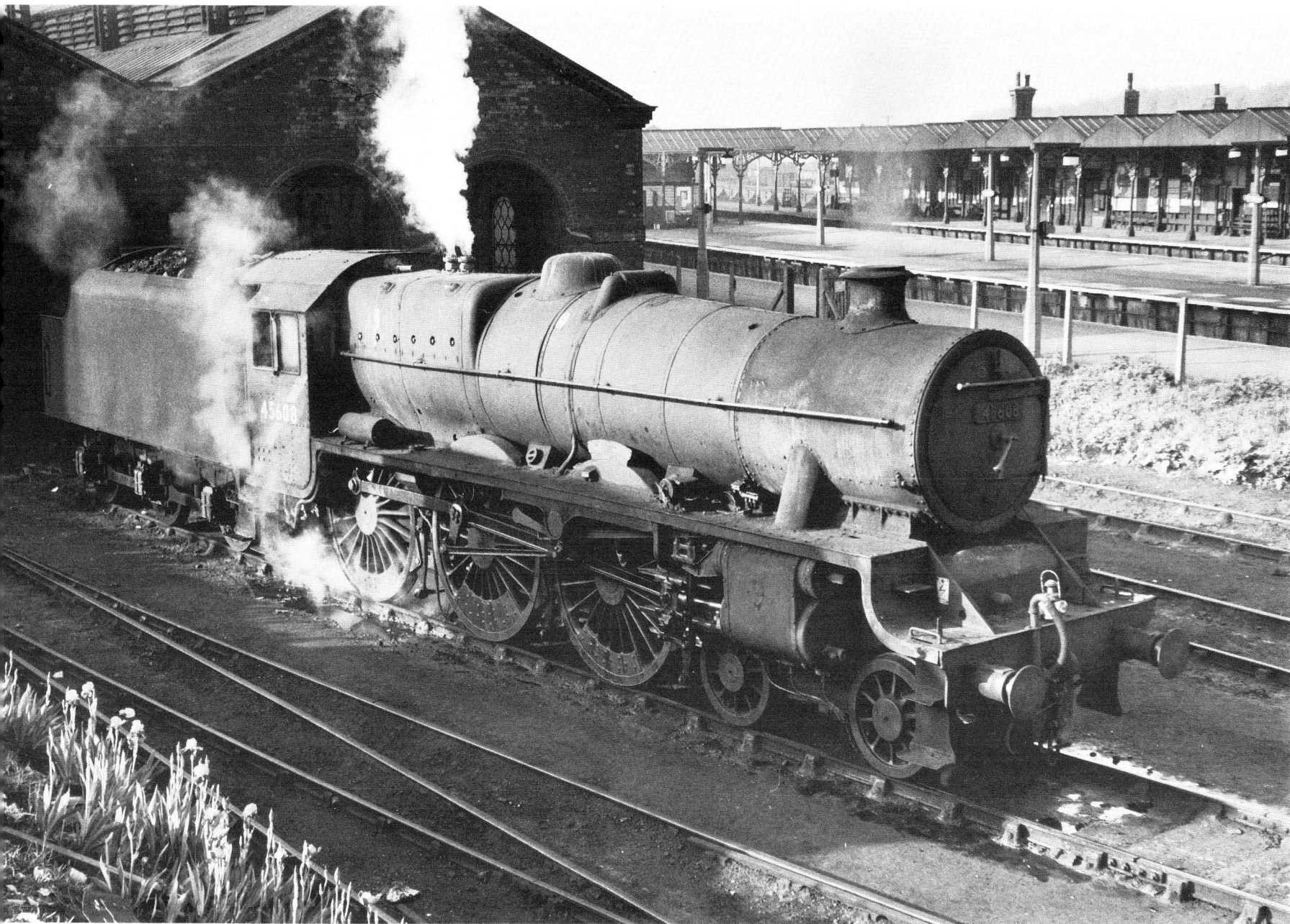

99. Almost the end at Kettering shed as Leeds (Holbeck) Jubilee class No. 45608 GIBRALTAR stands in No. 3 road, devoid of nameplates and looking a little the worse for wear. The four road shed was typical of the Midland architecture for the period when opened in 1876 with ornamental brickwork and arched openings – it finally closed on 13 June 1965, and demolition followed soon after. The Jubilee engine was also withdrawn in September of the same year. However Kettering station in the background has changed very little, and today retains a lot of its old Midland Railway character. (M. Winnett)

100. A view of the shed yard at Kettering from Northfield Avenue, the approach road to Kettering station. 8F class No. 48177 leaves the shed to begin another turn of duty, while a magnificent smoke screen spreads over the sky as a northbound train climbs the 1 in 132 rising gradient towards Glendon South Junction. Class 4F No. 44156 stands out of steam to witness the spectacle. (W. J. S. Meredith)

101. Kettering station signal box situated to the south of the station witnesses a busy evening scene during the summer of 1961. Fowler 2-6-4 tank No. 42331 from Leicester shed, waits to take back a local Kettering to Leicester train – a service normally worked by a Leicester locomotive. Meanwhile in the background a Wellingborough to Corby evening freight train passes, with 4F class No. 44575 and 9F class 92112 in control. This was a regular local evening train and was known as Trip No. 12 (or Target 12) from Wellingborough shed, and one of the two locomotives always ran tender first. (L. W. Roy)

102. A Kettering-based class 4F locomotive thrashes up the bank past Glendon South Junction signal box, and heads towards Corby with a Manton 'pick-up' freight from Kettering up sidings during the spring of 1959. Of particular interest is the positioning of the signal box between the fast and slow lines. From inside the signal box trains heading south on the fast line would appear to be 'coming through the windows' being at the same level, and in fact coal from well filled tenders would quite regularly fall and break the windows at that end of the signal box, as the trains rushed down the falling gradient towards Kettering. Needless to say the vibration of passing trains also considerably shook the structure! (Tony Heighton)

Left: 103. Jubilee class No. 45612 JAMAICA storms up the final few yards of the long three mile 1 in 160 climb from Kettering station, with a northbound express via Manton on a sunny day in the 1950s. The picture, taken from the steps of Glendon South Junction signal box, clearly shows both the slow and fast lines of the Midland main line. Up until late 1987 the stretch of railway from St. Pancras to Glendon North Junction had the distinction of being the longest continuous four track line in Britain, even though the two pairs of lines separated between Souldrop Box and Irchester South Junction (about three miles), the slow lines passing through Sharnbrook Tunnel (one mile long). *(P. I. Rawlinson)*

Above: 104. Driver Betts and fireman Winnett take a breather during ballast train duties at Glendon South Junction on Sunday, 11 February 1962, with a shabby looking Wellingborough-based 8F class No. 48381. *(M. Winnett collection)*

MIDLAND MAIN LINE
BEDFORD TO MARKET HARBOROUGH
AND HARRINGWORTH

Left: 105. Kettering Ivatt class No. 46444 shunts the old goods yard at Glendon and Rushton station during the summer of 1959. Iron ore was brought in by lorries from the Nassington–Barrowden Mining Company quarries, and was tipped into wagons. Once filled, the wagons would be marshalled and then hauled to Shelton, Stoke-on-Trent via a Glendon to Burslem working.
(Tony Heighton)

Opposite top: 106. One of the Midland main line's top link expresses, 'The Thames-Clyde Express', linking London with Glasgow, powers through Glendon and Rushton station at the start of the three mile climb up Desborough bank during the summer of 1959. Leeds (Holbeck) Black 5 No. 44852 provides the power with Leicester, the first stop, still some 23 miles away. The complete journey time took just over ten hours!
(Tony Heighton)

MIDLAND MAIN LINE
BEDFORD TO
MARKET HARBOROUGH
AND HARRINGWORTH

Left: 107. Black 5 No. 44944 pulls into Glendon and Rushton station with the 6.53 p.m. stopping train to Leicester on the evening of Monday, 6 July 1959. On 4 January 1960 the station was closed to passengers, but goods traffic continued to use the station for a further five years. *(Tony Heighton)*

Below: 108. 8F class No. 48635 brings a special freight down Desborough bank into Desborough and Rothwell station on Sunday, 5 May 1963, past a Midland Railway '2 doll' bracket signal with splitting distant (i.e. the home signal could be used together with either distant). In the background can be seen the high water tank that supplies Desborough with water. Although the station was situated in Desborough, the station name suggests Desborough and Rothwell, even though Rothwell was over one mile away! The station finally closed 1 January 1968. *(P. I. Rawlinson)*

MIDLAND MAIN LINE
BEDFORD TO MARKET HARBOROUGH AND HARRINGWORTH

Left: 109. An example of the gas lamp and station totem sign at Desborough and Rothwell station on 5 May 1963. *(P. I. Rawlinson)*

DESBOROUGH
& ROTHWELL

110. The north end of Market Harborough in the summer of 1950, showing the many wagons parked in the yards both sides of the main line, with Market Harborough No. 2 signal box just off the end of the station platforms. Rugby-based Midland 2F No. 58269 is serviced in the shed yard. Although not on the Midland main line, Rugby shed always supplied locomotives to Market Harborough until 1955. (R. J. Rawlinson)

111. The girder footbridge at Great Bowden was a favourite place for young trainspotters to stand and get wonderfully dirty by the smoke and steam from trains that passed underneath. In this view on the Saturday afternoon of 16 February 1957, Fowler 4F No. 44110 makes its way towards Market Harborough, on the line from Peterborough with a train of military equipment. It is being rapidly overhauled however by Compound 4-4-0 No. 41185, acting as pilot to Standard 4-6-0 No. 73144, as they rush past with their St. Pancras bound express on the up main line. *(R. Gammage)*

112. Later the same afternoon, from the opposite side of the footbridge, shadows lengthen as Stanier Jubilee No. 45610 GOLD COAST works away from Market Harborough, gathering speed past Great Bowden recreation ground, as she heads towards her home town of Derby. The clear winter air and low sun create the mood.
(R. Gammage)

BEDFORD TO
MARKET HARBOROUGH
AND HARRINGWORTH

113. A dramatic view of two trains on the Kettering furnaces' narrow gauge railway system at Rothwell pit. On the left KETTERING FURNACES No. 7 0-6-0ST, built by Manning Wardle in 1897, waits in the sidings, while KETTERING FURNACES No. 8 0-6-0ST, also built by Manning Wardle but in 1906, brings out a load of iron ore bound for the furnaces. The locomotives were always kept in beautiful external condition. *(Tony Heighton)*

114. The Kettering Coal and Iron Co. Ltd. operated an extensive three foot gauge system to bring iron ore from their quarries to the furnaces, which were situated adjacent to the Midland main line, one and a half miles north of Kettering station. In this view KETTERING FURNACES No. 2 0-4-0ST, built by Black and Hawthorn in 1879, shunts a train of ore onto the tipping dock during 1958. Although the furnaces finally ceased production from 24 April 1959, the narrow gauge continued in operation until 24 October 1962 to remove further reserves of iron ore which, after being tipped into B.R. tipplers, were sent by rail to Corby steelworks. *(Tony Heighton)*

Opposite: 115. What a marvellous rural setting showing the true character of an industrial railway, as KETTERING FURNACES No. 2 ambles through the Northamptonshire countryside with an iron ore train during 1958. At this time the Kettering system was the oldest ironstone tramway in use, in substantially original form, and certainly No. 2 was the oldest locomotive to work on the railway. It arrived new in 1879 and incredibly was still hard at work when the furnaces closed 80 years later! Of particular note is the open cab on No. 2, with the spectacled weatherboard turned over at the top – hardly offering the crew much protection in adverse weather conditions. *(Tony Heighton)*

Above: 116. A rare view inside Gretton Brook locomotive shed at Corby during 1959. The shed opened in August 1954, and had eight parallel roads capable of holding forty industrial locomotives. It was built solely for use by the quarry locomotives, and was one of the biggest industrial sheds in the country. The Stewarts and Lloyds steelwork locomotives remained within their own complex. In this view Kitson-built locomotives, which arrived in the 1930s, surround No. 57 in the foreground, which arrived brand new in 1950, built by Robert Stephenson and Hawthorns Ltd. *(Tony Heighton)*

117. A general view of the Corby steelworks complex, showing the extensive railway system within the works, as well as the opencast quarries in the Weldon area, on the 16 August 1937. In later years it was to have the largest ironstone tramway system in North-amptonshire. The whole area measured some one and a half miles by three quarters of a mile, and was accompanied by considerable activity in the adjacent quarries where some of the biggest excavators in the world were at work. It is also of note that the existence of iron ore in the area was first revealed in the cutting of the Midland Railway between Corby and Gretton in the 1870s. (*Aerofilms Ltd.*)

118. One of the thirty or so steelworks locomotives at Corby, No. 16, a Hawthorn Leslie built 0-6-0ST, has a break in shunting duties while the footplate crew have a chat. No. 16 arrived new in October 1934, and was formerly numbered S & L 11. This picture taken in 1959 shows the loco painted in golden yellow, an experimental colour, in order to make it more easily seen in the drab steelworks surroundings! The experiment obviously worked, as others were painted in similar colours in later months.
(Tony Heighton)

119. Kettering-based Stanier 8F No. 48069 shunts No. 10 road (known as the cripple wagon road) at the exchange sidings at the Stewarts and Lloyds Corby steelworks during 1952. The four blast furnaces that worked from 1934 to their closure in 1980 form an imposing backdrop. *(British Steel, Tubes Division, Corby)*

120. A dramatic night view of the Corby steelworks complex, showing that the industrial establishment worked seven days a week, twenty-four hours a day.
(*M. Goddard-Jackson N.R.O. ref ZB 702/11*)

Opposite top: 122. A Fowler 2-6-4 tank scampers across the magnificent Welland Viaduct and crosses the county boundary into Rutland (as it was then) with a local train from Kettering to Leicester during the autumn of 1959. The viaduct is the longest masonry viaduct across a valley in Britain, and was opened by the Midland Railway in 1880. It stretches for nearly three quarters of a mile, stands sixty feet above the river, and its eighty-two arches required fifteen million bricks which were all especially manufactured at nearby Seaton. Situated next to Harringworth village, it provides Northamptonshire with one of the finest monuments to Victorian railway engineering to be found in the country. *(Tony Heighton)*

Above: 121. Dusk falls over the Welland Valley as a class 8F hauled freight train clanks off Welland Viaduct, and begins the two mile 1 in 167 climb up to Manton, bound for the coalfields of Nottinghamshire. In the foreground the Stamford to Seaton and Uppingham to Seaton lines meet and lead to Seaton Junction, recognisable by its array of semaphore signals. *(Tony Heighton)*

Opposite bottom: 123. A Nottingham-bound express hauled by a Jubilee class locomotive heads across Welland Viaduct on the evening of 7 July 1959. *(Tony Heighton)*

MIDLAND BYWAYS

Left: 124. Veteran ex-G.E.R. J15 class No. 65461, a Cambridge locomotive, stands in platform 3 at Kettering station, having just arrived with the first train of the day from Cambridge during the summer of 1957. Normal practice at this time was for the locomotive to spend the day at Kettering carrying out shunting duties, and then work the last train back to Cambridge, departing at 5.20 p.m. *(Tony Heighton)*

Below: 125. The end of the Varsity line! Passengers from the last Cambridge to Kettering train mingle at Kettering station on Saturday, 13 June 1959. Emblazoned with chalked slogans, Kettering's Ivatt No. 46496 stands in the evening sunshine, the centre of attraction, with driver Maxey and fireman Freeman basking in the limelight on the footplate. *(Tony Heighton)*

KETTERING TO CAMBRIDGE

Above: 126. Kettering's Ivatt class No. 46404 eases past Kettering Junction signal box with the 2.10 p.m. Kettering to Cambridge train on Monday, 7 April 1958. These locomotives were first allocated to Kettering, especially to work on the Cambridge line, in 1947 when Nos. 6400-2 arrived. The single line working tablet can just be seen disappearing through the cab window as the driver works his short train onto the branch. The signal box was different from the basic Midland style, and was built in L.M.S. days with L.N.W.R. influence in the design. *(Tony Heighton)*

Opposite bottom: 128. The afternoon Cambridge train from Kettering approaches Cranford station behind one of the regular Kettering locomotives, Ivatt class No. 46496, during April 1958. A solitary car travels along the A604 Kettering to Huntingdon road, while in the foreground the redundant chimney from the long-gone Clay Cross Iron Company, which worked from 1913 to 1926, overlooks the railway. *(Tony Heighton)*

Left: 127. Standard class 2 No. 78020 puts on a sprint up the steep 1 in 70 'Butlin's Bank' as it climbs away from the Midland main line at Kettering Junction with the 2.10 p.m. Kettering to Cambridge train on Saturday, 22 March 1958. Wicksteed Park now covers a large part of the background landscape. *(Tony Heighton)*

Above: 129. A pleasant branch line view at Cranford station on Saturday, 10 May 1958 as Ivatt No. 46496 ambles through with the 2.10 p.m. Kettering to Cambridge train. The station had alas already closed to passengers some two years earlier on 2 April 1956, and finally closed to goods traffic from 6 November 1961. However, the nearby ironstone quarry continued producing iron ore for a number of years, and no doubt many of their workers called into the *Red Lion* for refreshment. *(Tony Heighton)*

Opposite: 130. A bitterly cold north-easterly wind sweeps across the exposed Raunds station in the Nene Valley during Saturday, 23 February 1957. The overnight frost is still well in evidence as ex-G.E.R. J15 class No. 65475 brings the 7.25 a.m. Cambridge to Kettering to rest for the handful of passengers. Raunds was a good example of the isolated nature of the stations along the Kettering–Cambridge line, and was some two miles from the village. No wonder bus travel became a more convenient way of travelling. *(Ian L. Wright)*

MIDLAND BYWAYS
KETTERING TO CAMBRIDGE

131. Another Kettering-based Ivatt class No. 46444 waits for departure time at Thrapston Midland Road station, with the 8.25 a.m. Kettering to Cambridge train during May 1959. For many years the Kettering to Cambridge line had a service of three trains each way a day. The thirty-three mile route ran through sparsely populated countryside with many stations being badly sited. The single line had severe gradients and sharp curves, and consequently the trains were slow. The decline of the line was gradual, and it finally closed to passenger traffic the following month despite vigorous opposition. *(Tony Heighton)*

MIDLAND BYWAYS

132. Grafham station on the last day of passenger service, 13 June 1959. A glorious summer's day, and young and old pay their last respects to a railway line that never really stood a chance against the modern world of cars and buses. Full trains were the order of the day and the very last one, the 8.10 p.m. Kettering to Cambridge, carried more than one hundred and fifty passengers! (*Tony Heighton*)

KETTERING TO CAMBRIDGE

Above: 133. At Wellingborough Midland Road station on Saturday, 2 May 1959, Stanier Black 5 No. 44816 prepares to pull its coaches out from the sidings and back down into the station, in readiness to haul the local stopping train to Leicester, due out at 4.58 p.m. On the opposite side of the tracks a Johnson 0-4-4 tank No. 58080 busies herself, pulling empty coaches into the station for working the Higham branch. *(L. W. Roy)*

Left/below: 134/135. Ivatt class 2 No. 41328 from Wellingborough shed draws the two Higham coaches out of their sidings, and enters platform 5 at Wellingborough Midland Road station with an afternoon train to Rushden and Higham Ferrers. Wellingborough station signal box, dating from 1893, stands proud at the end of the platforms at the north end of the station in this 1959 scene. It was finally dismantled in 1988. *(Tony Heighton)*

MIDLAND BYWAYS WELLINGBOROUGH TO HIGHAM FERRERS

Right: 137. Wellingborough 4F class No. 43929 approaches Irchester Junction with the return daily branch freight from Wellingborough, picking up and delivering goods at both Rushden and Higham Ferrers stations. In this scene on Saturday, 8 August 1960, the number 11 can be seen on the front of the locomotive signifying that this is Trip No. 11 from Wellingborough shed, one of the regular local freight trips in the area. It was February 1969 when the last freight train ran on the branch. (*R. A. F. Puryer*)

Opposite top: 136. The Higham branch line train runs past a pair of ex-Midland Railway semaphore signals behind Ivatt class 2 No. 41328, and approaches Irchester Junction signal box where the signalman leans out to hand over the single line working token to the fireman. Up to as many as fourteen trips were made up the branch every weekday, but no service ran on a Sunday. The view in this picture is of the 8.09 p.m. Wellingborough to Higham train during the final year of passenger service in 1959. *(P.I.Rawlinson)*

Below: 138. The Higham branch was mainly worked by two coach, push-and-pull sets, but during 1952 a 'Saturdays only' through working from Higham to Leicester was introduced. This train was often loaded to nine or ten coaches, and only just fitted into the station loop at Higham station, thus allowing the locomotive, which came up tender first on the 11.25 a.m. from Wellingborough, to run round its train. On a very pleasant Saturday in January 1956, Stanier Black 5 No. 44825 shows signs of impatience, standing in the rural setting among the cabbages, awaiting the 11.57 a.m. departure time. *(Ian L. Wright)*

Left: 139. This photograph brings to mind Don Breckon's well known painting 'Racing the Train', as the boy endeavours to outrun the 'Saturdays only' Leicester train, before it pulls to a stop at Rushden station. On this occasion in September 1958 it was hauled by Kentish Town Jubilee No. 45712 VICTORY. A Jubilee on the branch was unheard of, and this may well have been the only time it occurred. *(P. I. Rawlinson)*

Right: 140. There is no age barrier in the enthusiasm for the steam locomotive and railways in general. Here we have, against a backdrop of 1958 Rushden, a man and boy gazing in admiration at Jubilee No. 45712 VICTORY, gently easing her train away round the curve towards Wellingborough and Leicester. *(P. I. Rawlinson)*

MIDLAND BYWAYS
WELLINGBOROUGH TO
HIGHAM FERRERS

141. Saturday, 13 June 1959 and the last day of passenger services on the Higham branch, although one would hardly think so looking at the immaculate condition of Higham station.
(L. Hanson)

142. The same immaculate conditions are found at Rushden as Standard 2-6-2 tank No. 84007, performing its push-and-pull role sandwiched in between a couple of two-coach sets, prepares for departure.
(L. Hanson)

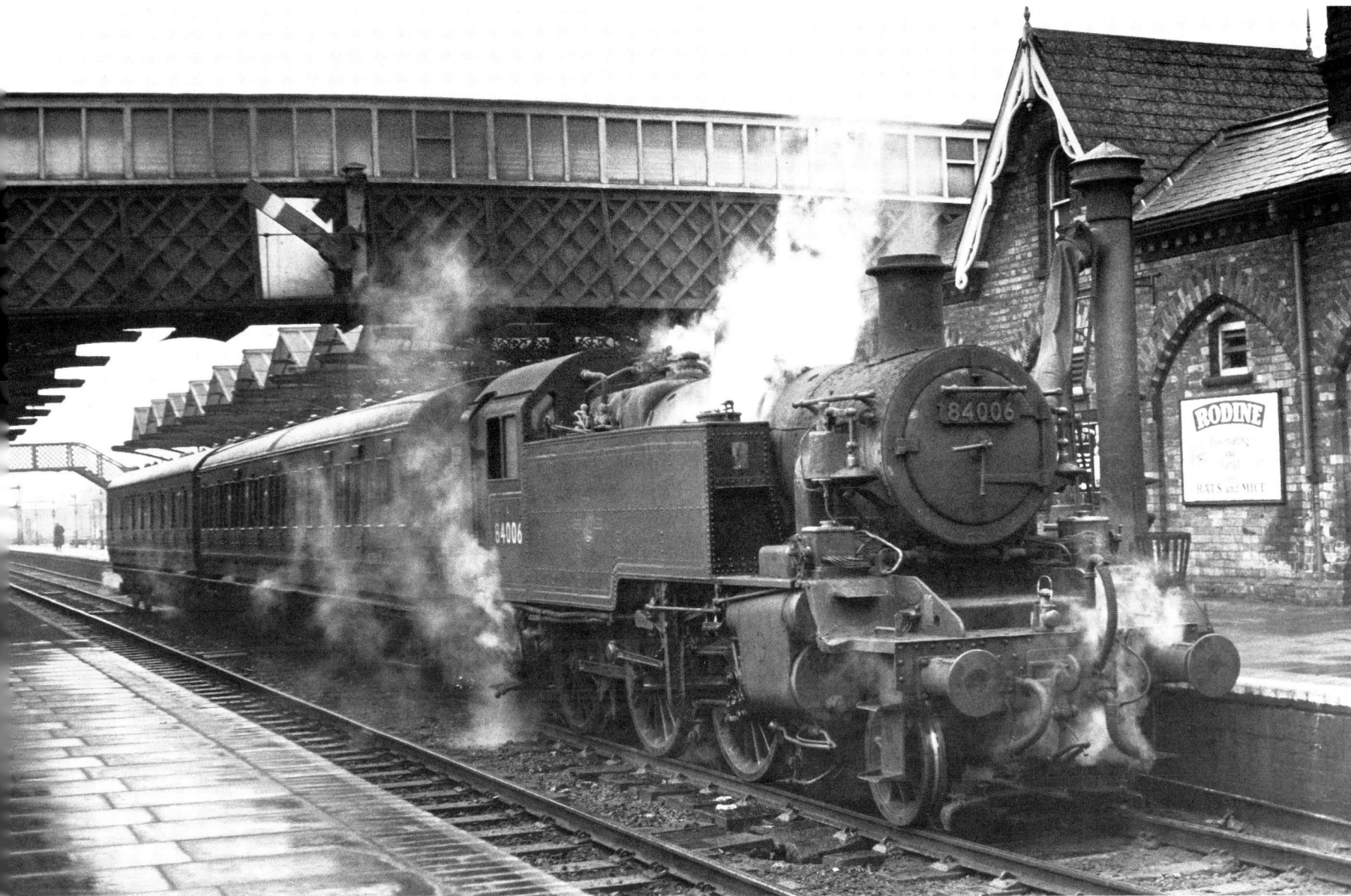

143. Standard class 2 tank No. 84006 stands at Bedford Midland Road station, having just arrived with the 4.00 p.m. train from Northampton on Thursday, 15 February 1962. No doubt the passengers from Northampton, Piddington, Olney and Turvey will be rather reluctant to leave their warm steam-heated coaches, and venture out into the dismal wet weather. At this time the station still retained much of its Midland Railway character, later to be lost in a rebuilding scheme. Passenger services on the line finally ended on 3 March 1962. *(K. Fairey)*

Right: 144. From the cab of Ivatt 2-6-2 tank No. 41228, fireman Brian Busby prepares to hand the single line working token to Turvey signalman Aubrey Wilkens on Thursday, 15 February 1962. The Northampton to Bedford line was double track throughout, but with closure to passenger traffic less than a month away it was only being worked as a single line at this time. Turvey signal box was a typical Midland Railway wooden structure, with hipped roof. *(K. Fairey)*

Left: 145. No. 41228 works away from Olney station during the same trip, and fireman Busby is about to take the token from signalman Ted Allsopp. The original wooden signal box at Olney had been replaced by an L.M.S. version, with brick base and gable ended roof. *(K. Fairey)*

Above: 146. In the crisp cold winter air, Patriot class No. 45533 Lord Rathmore in spotless condition, and grimy Northampton 4F class No. 44219, make a most impressive sight as they shatter the peace of the quiet branch line station at Turvey, with a football special from Northampton to Luton on Saturday, 7 January 1961. This was the last time a Patriot class locomotive worked over this particular line. *(R. A. F. Puryer)*

MIDLAND BYWAYS: BEDFORD TO NORTHAMPTON

Opposite: 147. The River Ouse at Olney has overflowed its banks once again, flooding the surrounding meadows on Thursday, 6 February 1951. In this view looking towards Warrington and Lavendon Grange, an ex-Midland Fowler 4F 0-6-0 works away from Olney towards Bedford, with its through freight, appropriately crossing over the flood bridge. *(Aerofilms Ltd.)*

Opposite top: 148. Bedford-based Standard 2-6-2 tank No. 84005 arrives at the lonely outpost of Piddington on Thursday, 15 February 1962. The station master *cum* general factotum waits in anticipation just in case a passenger gets off. No one does, and a few minutes later with a short blast of the whistle and the photographer on board, 84005 hurries her train on towards the next stop at Olney. *(K. Fairey)*

Below: 150. May 1939 finds Fowler Midland 4F No. 3977 simmering gently at Northampton St. John's Street station, having arrived some time earlier with its local passenger train. This fine view gives a glimpse of the station's architecture. The advertisements on the far left are on the corner of Fetter Street, and the signal box (right background) is adjacent to the bridge over Victoria Promenade. The station closed to passenger and freight traffic two months later, so ending the separate Midland link into the town. *(W. J. S. Meredith)*

Opposite bottom: 149. Piddington station about six years earlier and, apart from the differently designed station nameboard, the situation is basically the same, as Ivatt tank No. 41270 prepares to propel its train towards Northampton. It is a mystery why it was called Piddington station at all, with the villages of Horton and Hackleton both being nearer than Piddington, which was some two and a half miles away. *(J. Harrison)*

MIDLAND BYWAYS
BEDFORD TO NORTHAMPTON

THE COUNTY TOWN: NORTHAMPTON

Above: 152. The wet cobbles of the goods warehouse yard at Northampton Castle reflect the gas lamps from within, silhouetting the drays on this dismal night late in 1935. *(L Hanson)*

Right: 153. Nineteen years later things have changed very little, as Arthur Jones and Ray Clarke prepare to leave the yard with timber carriage, horse and chain horse at the end of February 1954. *(J. Harrison)*

Opposite: 151. Workmen and passengers laugh and chat on this beautiful summer's day, as work proceeds replacing the forecourt canopy at Castle station on 12 July 1939. Two months later World War II was declared. *(W. J. S. Meredith)*

Left: 154. After clattering over the cobbles in the goods yard, the draymen lead their horses and loaded timber carriage out towards the *Travis and Arnold* depot on the other side of West Bridge. *(J. Harrison)*

THE
COUNTY TOWN
NORTHAMPTON

Below: 155. Castle station frontage and forecourt in August 1964. *(W. J. S. Meredith)*

156. Bertram Mills Circus arrives by special train at Northampton Castle on Sunday, 1 June 1952. Camels disembark at the fish dock, and are prepared for the parade with the other large animals, through the town to the big top. This was the last time the circus arrived by train, although it still used the station yard to congregate the animals before parades in later years. (*J. Harrison*)

157. The Inspection Department at British Timken used to organise its own private annual outing to the coast, chartering a train from British Railways for the occasion. The summer 1961 trip to Margate stands at platform 1, behind an unidentified Northampton Black 5. With the boiler pressure already at 225 p.s.i. she is ready for departure as the clock, coincidentally next to a Timken advertisement, ticks on to 7.36 a.m. (P. Martin)

L. M. S. R. P.F.70.

NORTHAMPTON

158. Luggage label.

THE COUNTY TOWN: NORTHAMPTON

159. A rebuilt Claud Hamilton class D16/3 4-4-0 No. 62535 shedded at Peterborough (Spital Bridge), waits in bay platform 5 at Northampton Castle with the 12.30 p.m. stopping train to Peterborough on Saturday, 17 July 1954. At this time this type of locomotive was regularly used on the Peterborough trains, and was one of the few ex-L.N.E.R. classes to appear at the station. Although the buildings on the right have disappeared, Northampton No. 1 signal box, as well as the bridge carrying the track bed over Foot Meadow, still remain today. *(Ross Smith)*

160. Northampton Chamber of Trade promoted a 'Bargain Week' in October 1937, organising various functions. The L.M.S. decided to contribute by putting on display, during Thursday, 14 October Royal Scot class 4-6-0 No. 6147 THE NORTHAMPTONSHIRE REGIMENT and, by contrast, the oldest locomotive working on the L.M.S. at that time, ex-Midland Railway 2-4-0 No. 20002 (now preserved as M.R.158A). The latter had covered over 1,500,000 miles since being built in 1866. There was also a train of modern coaching stock on view, all in bay platforms 2 and 3. Here we see a school party arriving for a guided tour. (W. J. S. Meredith)

THE COUNTY TOWN: NORTHAMPTON

161. Viewing of the locomotives was limited to the footplate, but boys being boys climb everywhere they are not supposed to. Eventually a friendly constable of the Railway Police endeavours to restore some sort of order to the occasion.
(W. J. S. Meredith)

162. A regular feature of summer Saturdays in the 1930s was the 'Tea Party Special'. This was a train booked by an organization, usually a Sunday School, for taking parties of children out for the day. Usually only a short trip to Blisworth, Billing, Piddington etc. was made, the empty train then returning to Northampton. Later the same day it returned to pick up the party. The children would walk, often to a nearby field, where games were organized, tea was laid on, and a good time was had by one and all, free of charge. In this photograph an unusual locomotive has been commandeered for the short trip on Saturday, 7 July 1934 in the form of Bowen-Cooke class 3P 4-6-2 tank No. 6984. A train hardly warranting express passenger head lamp code. (L. Hanson)

163. Children on a 'Tea Party Special' gaze out from the carriage as they await departure on Saturday, 22 July 1933. According to the photographer's notebook, two of the girls are Alice Shipley and Cissy Bowne. *(W. J. S. Meredith)*

164. Mr. Bill Ward prepares to board a train standing in the Rugby bay at Castle station on Saturday, 6 April 1929. *(W. J. S. Meredith)*

165. Railway employees pose in the doorway of the first-class compartment of coach No. 3396 on Saturday, 14 September 1929, at Northampton Castle. *(W. J. S. Meredith)*

Above: 166. Still on the winter timetable early in 1952, Rugby Black 5 No. 45429 awaits departure from platform 1 with a Rugby to Bletchley local, due out at 10.23 a.m. This train waited for a connection at Rugby, which is probably the reason for it being late. The platform layout with its array of signs, mainly from L.N.W.R. days, will have changed little since the station was built in 1881. *(R. J. Rawlinson)*

THE COUNTY TOWN: NORTHAMPTON

Right: 167. Not much 'Rest Assured' for fireman Norman Quennell – he will be shovelling coal into the firebox of Fowler Patriot No. 45533 LORD RATHMORE many times after leaving platform 1 before he gets to Euston. *(L. W. Roy)*

Opposite: 168. Station foreman Charlie Braybrook marches down platform 6 at Northampton Castle station, obviously not sharing the enthusiasm of the many local railway enthusiasts who are joining the Derby Works Open Day special train on Saturday, 29 August 1959, hauled by Rugby Black 5 No. 44863. Always a memorable annual occasion for trainspotters, the Derby Works trip was a chance to be allowed to wander round the works and shed at Derby without restriction, and see some 200–300 steam locomotives! One wonders what the two elderly ladies are discussing on the opposite platform! *(George Smith)*

169. Eager Northampton holiday-makers swarm onto platform 1 at Northampton Castle station, as the London train arrives behind Standard class 4 No. 75052, a Willesden locomotive, to take them south at the beginning of the factory fortnight in July 1960. *(L. W. Roy)*

THE COUNTY TOWN: NORTHAMPTON

Above: 170. It is amazing just how much a chimney can alter a locomotive's appearance, and the double chimney on Stanier Jubilee No. 45742 CONNAUGHT completely spoilt its looks. Not only that, it apparently did nothing to improve efficiency, subsequently reverting back to single chimney form in 1955. In this view from Northampton No. 1 signal box, CONNAUGHT pulls out from platform 1 and swings across the tracks, making for London via Roade with the 9.45 a.m. Wolverhampton to Euston express on Whit Sunday, 6 June 1954. *(Ross Smith)*

Right: 171. Signalman Glover stands at the 54 level frame inside Northampton No. 1 signal box on 6 March 1955. Mr. Glover worked this box for seventeen years. *(Ross Smith)*

Opposite: 172. A superb landscape view from West Bridge overlooking Foot Meadow. Class 8F No. 48332 heads home with coal empties for Toton, Nottingham as it coasts past Northampton No. 1 signal box down the 1 in 200 gradient on Saturday, 21 October 1961. Duckweed covers the River Nene, while in the background the view across Far Cotton shows the gas works, carriage shed, coaling stage at the shed, and the destructor plant at the corporation depot – all familiar landmarks that have now disappeared. *(L. W. Roy)*

Opposite: 173. The afternoon Rugby to Euston train climbs the bank away from Northampton towards Roade, at around 4.20 p.m., hauled by Black 5 No. 44915 on this beautiful spring day in 1961. Stanier Black 5s were known to locomotive crews as the 'Engineman's Friend', for they were grand machines to fire and drive, seldom temperamental however badly they were treated. Combined with sure footedness and a good turn of speed, it was hardly surprising that locomotive crews were happy when they knew a Black 5 had been rostered to them. *(L. W. Roy)*

Above: 174. Ex -L.N.W.R. 'Super D' No. 49361 propels its ballast train across from the down line to the up, while on Sunday track maintenance work on 6 March 1955. This signal box view shows the reverse curves up to '15 arches' viaduct, with Duston West beyond where the Roade line crosses the Blisworth branch. *(Ross Smith)*

175. Standard class 2 tank No. 84006 waits in bay platform 4 at Castle station, on the 4.00 p.m. train to Bedford on Thursday, 15 February 1962, as the fireman prepares to water the locomotive. In just over two weeks time the last Northampton to Bedford train will run on 3 March 1962, and yet another passenger branch line in the area will be axed. Today, although the watering column and semaphore signal have gone, this part of the platform remains, as does Northampton No. 1 signal box. *(K. Fairey)*

176. Caught in the act! One of the photographers represented in this book leans out of the window of Northampton No. 1 signal box for a better view of Stanier Coronation Pacific No. 46221 QUEEN ELIZABETH, entering Castle station with her diverted Euston to Glasgow express on Sunday, 31 May 1959. *(R. A. F. Puryer)*

THE COUNTY TOWN: NORTHAMPTON

177. From his low vantage point the boy gazes in wonderment at the formidable size of Stanier Coronation Pacific No. 46231 Duchess of Atholl, as the bridge above Foot Meadow vibrates under her 161 tons of mobile metal. The fireman smiles as the Sunday diverted 'Royal Scot' runs into Castle station on 23 July 1950.

Duchess of Atholl is painted in the early British Railways lined blue livery, originally proposed for large express passenger locomotives, but subsequently abandoned in favour of Brunswick green. (L. Hanson)

TRAIN
COMING

178. Looking under West Bridge on Monday, 6 August 1962, Stanier Coronation Pacific No. 46246 CITY OF MANCHESTER awaits departure from platform 1, with the afternoon Llandudno to Euston train. Crossing the tracks with a trolley of parcels used to be a precarious occupation for the porters. Down trains could not be seen coming through the bridge until the last minute. On one occasion this resulted in a train hitting a trolley of shoes, scattering them in all directions. To prevent further occurrences 'Train Coming' signs were fixed each side of the bridge. These worked in conjunction with an electrical track circuit, and lit up when a train entered the sections surrounding Castle station, thus giving advance warning of the train's arrival. (G. R. Onley)

THE COUNTY TOWN: NORTHAMPTON

Above: 179. Obtaining the all clear through the centre road at Castle station, Toton 8F No. 48194 opens out past No. 2 signal box, gathering as much speed as possible to charge the bank towards Roade with her rake of coal wagons during the summer of 1961. *(L. W. Roy)*

THE COUNTY TOWN: NORTHAMPTON

Opposite bottom: 181. Looking quite resplendent in lined-out crimson lake livery, and rather out of character on a freight working, large boilered Claughton No. 6004 leaves the north end of Castle station in December 1936. No. 6004 was one of three large boilered Claughtons shedded at Northampton from January to October 1935 for working the 'Crewe turn', a mileage job by No. 1 link (the others being 5993 and 5999 VINDICTIVE). When No. 6004 first arrived at Northampton she was named PRINCESS LOUISE, but her nameplates were removed later that year, and the name transferred to new Princess Royal Pacific No. 6204. *(W. J. S. Meredith)*

Left: 180. Nicknamed the 'Turbomotive' by railway enthusiasts, steam-turbine driven Princess Royal Pacific No. 6202 enters the north end of Castle station, running light engine from Crewe works back to its home shed at Camden, during December 1936. Expensive to maintain, mainly owing to its uniqueness, it spent a lot of time in works, and was eventually re-built as a conventionally driven locomotive in August 1952. Then named PRINCESS ANNE she was smashed beyond economic repair in the Harrow and Wealdstone crash two months later. *(W. J. S. Meredith)*

182. A gentleman admirer watches the massive proportions of Princess Royal Pacific No. 6206 PRINCESS MARIE LOUISE, working past Victoria Park with a down diverted express on Sunday, 26 September 1937. Locomotive and tender are in L.M.S. crimson lake livery. The twelve inch numerals and fourteen inch letters are gold, with vermilion red shading. *(W. J. S. Meredith)*

183. This familiar view from Victoria Park across the River Nene finds 'Baby Scot' (Patriot class) No. 5518 heading north from Castle station on Sunday, 25 October 1936. Built in 1933 this locomotive was named BRADSHAW in 1939. Like the rest of her class that remained in this original form (some were rebuilt with a larger taper boiler) she had her livery changed from crimson lake to Brunswick green after the formation of British Railways in 1948. Withdrawn from service in October 1962, BRADSHAW was cut up at Horwich Works in February 1963. (W. J. S. Meredith)

THE COUNTY TOWN: NORTHAMPTON

Below: 184. Rebuilt Patriot 4-6-0 No. 45545 PLANET powers her train out of Riverside platform 7 at Castle station during the winter of 1959. The cold air and low angle of the sun backlight her exhaust, creating this dramatic scene as she passes the signal gantry adjacent to Spencer Bridge. The spectacles at the bottom of the three left hand signal posts indicate that a call plunger is situated on the box at the foot of the gantry post; by pressing this the fireman would ring a bell in No. 2 signal box to remind the signalman that a train was waiting; the signalman in return had to acknowledge by ringing a buzzer on the box. If the acknowledgement was not received, the fireman then had to report in person to the signal box. *(L. W. Roy)*

THE COUNTY TOWN: NORTHAMPTON

Opposite: 185. Silhouetted against the late afternoon sky of Wednesday, 14 April 1954, a construction worker descends after a day's work on the new signal gantry adjacent to Spencer Bridge. The gantry was being constructed to replace the various array of existing ex-L.N.W.R. signals that can be seen on illustration No. 181. Viewed from Victoria Park, with St. Andrew's church in the background, a Fowler 4F patiently waits for clearance to proceed southwards. *(W. J. S. Meredith)*

186. Viewed from the opposite side of the tracks, also on 14 April 1954, Northampton-based Ivatt 2-6-2 tank No. 41218, in early British Railway's livery, pauses at the signals while shunting empty coaching stock. At ground level work proceeds on the gantry, in preparation to replace the last sets of L.N.W.R. signals that remain in the Northampton station area. Victoria Park has always provided the setting for local folk to watch the passing trains. By the railway fence a specially raised bench was constructed from where trainspotters could see the train numbers in safety and to this day the bench is in use. (W. J. S. Meredith)

187. The superb signal gantry near Spencer Bridge overlooks the entrance to Castle yard as 9F class No. 92163, from Kettering shed, strides out with a fitted freight of box vans for the north on Saturday, 21 October 1961. Alas the gantry, although built as late as 1954, was demolished in the mid-1960s as modernisation took hold. (L. W. Roy)

THE COUNTY TOWN: NORTHAMPTON

188. Saltley-based Black 5 No. 44981 runs past Northampton No. 3 signal box with the 9.35 a.m. local train to Bletchley during May 1964. In the background the houses on Spencer Estate overlook the extensive marshalling yard, which extends to Northampton No. 4 signal box. The spire of St. John the Baptist Church in Kingsthorpe dominates the background landscape. (V. A. Hatley)

189. Sunday morning activity at Mill Lane road bridge, Kings-thorpe, as work is carried out in earnest in preparation for the forthcoming electrification. Willesden-based 8F No. 48603, in poor external condition, is used on the electrification train in this view on 31 May 1964. Already some masts have been erected, and in the months ahead the whole scene will be radically changed as the electric locomotives replace the steam. *(R. A. F. Puryer)*

Above: 190. Near Northampton No. 5 signal box in Kingsthorpe, the Market Harborough and Rugby lines out of Northampton diverge. This late afternoon scene on Saturday, 23 November 1963 shows Toton-based 8F No. 48163 working gently onto the Market Harborough branch, with a train of coal empties bound for the Nottinghamshire coalfields. Amongst the semaphore signals and telegraph poles and wires, the spires of Holy Sepulchre and St. Andrew's churches are just visible. *(R. A. F. Puryer)*

Right: 191. The spire of the early Norman church of St. John the Baptist in Kingsthorpe makes an interesting comparison against the two sets of semaphore signals near Northampton No. 5 signal box, in this late evening picture on Wednesday, 3 June 1964. *(R. A. F. Puryer)*

192. With the sun highlighting her classic lines, Bowen-Cooke Claughton No. 5934 powers her way past Kingsthorpe towards Rugby, with the 12.05 p.m. Euston to Crewe train circa 1934. The flat-capped driver silhouetted in the cab window concentrates on the road, as he passes the point where the Market Harborough branch diverges with the Northampton loop. *(W. J. S. Meredith)*

TOWARDS THE WELLAND VALLEY

193. The rural aspect of a branch line is well in evidence at Kingsthorpe, as Bletchley 8F No. 48554 slowly approaches Northampton No. 5 signal box, with an empty iron ore train from the north via Market Harborough on Friday, 24 January 1964.
(R. A. F. Puryer)

NORTHAMPTON TO MARKET HARBOROUGH

194. Bletchley 8F class No. 48544 throws up a column of black smoke as it accelerates onto the Market Harborough branch on Thursday, 11 March 1965, with an iron ore train from the Blisworth quarries to Scunthorpe. The Market Harborough branch was an extremely useful route for freight traffic between north and south, especially for coal and iron ore traffic.
(R. A. F. Puryer)

TOWARDS THE WELLAND VALLEY
NORTHAMPTON TO MARKET HARBOROUGH

Opposite top: 196. The footplate man awaits the guard's signal to set Fairburn 2-6-4 tank No. 42673 on its way from Brixworth towards Market Harborough, during the summer of 1959. *(Tony Heighton)*

Above: 195. A superbly captured late afternoon picture of 9F class No. 92154, storming past the small signal box at Spratton level crossing, on the Spratton to Brixworth road, with a train of coal empties for Toton during the winter of 1959. This rare photograph conveys the typical sight of a train at a level crossing, which was such a common feature throughout Northamptonshire before such branch lines were closed. *(Tony Heighton)*

Opposite bottom: 198. In the cold winter air, steam wafts up from under the frames of Standard 2-6-2 tank No. 84007, standing at Brixworth station with a Northampton to Market Harborough train early in 1959. On the up platform, porter and general handyman Tommy Wright keeps an eye on things as No. 84007 prepares to depart. This was obviously a well kept station, even the oil lamps were clean and ready for use. Another interesting feature is the unusual moulding round the canopy of the wooden shelter, not at all typical of the area. *(J. Harrison)*

Below: 197. The 'Hawkseye' station nameboard, painted red with white letters and surround. *(Tony Heighton)*

BRIXWORTH

199. Industrial steam steaming through Northamptonshire once again, this time in the Brixworth area. Scaldwell ironstone quarries were served by both three foot gauge and standard gauge railway systems. Here one of the standard gauge locomotives HARTINGTON, an 0-6-0ST built by the Avonside Engine Co. in 1921, crosses the Brixworth to Scaldwell road (with no crossing gates!) on route to the B.R. exchange sidings between Lamport and Brixworth, on the Northampton-Market Harborough line. The standard gauge line from Hanging Houghton to Scaldwell was laid as late as 1954 to replace a ropeway system. *(Tony Heighton)*

200. At the Scaldwell quarries the narrow gauge continued to serve as a 'feeder' to the standard gauge, and was about two miles in length. Iron ore would be brought up from the pits and be tipped into the standard gauge wagons. LAMPORT , an 0-6-0ST built by Pecketts, arrived new in 1913 and was one of four narrow gauge locomotives. In this incredibly rural scene it brings its short train of iron ore under the Brixworth to Holcot road, and threads its way through the vegetation on its three-quarter-mile trip to Scaldwell. The engine was completely overhauled in 1953, and looks a real picture with green paint, red coupling rods, red-backed nameplate, and a highly polished brass dome. *(Tony Heighton)*

Above: 201. Half a mile south of Lamport at the lonely Isham farm crossing stands a small cottage, where from a bedroom window a boy points his camera, waiting to photograph rebuilt Royal Scot No. 46100 ROYAL SCOT, on 28 April 1962. He knew it would be passing sometime soon because his father, who was the signalman at Lamport, told him it had gone through to Wembley on a special that morning. With sun and hope fading fast, she suddenly came storming round the curve, her crew piling on the power, anxious to get back to their home shed at Derby. Click went the shutter, the cottage shook as ROYAL SCOT pounded by, followed by the rhythm of carriage wheels on track joints, that gradually faded into the gathering dusk as the train disappeared towards Market Harborough. *(A. Briddon)*

202. 'Hawkseye' station nameboard and oil lamp at Lamport, 1959. *(Tony Heighton)*

Above: 203. An L.M.S. station nameboard in near original condition, with a golden-yellow beaded glass effect background; the letters and surround were black. *(Tony Heighton)*

Above: 204. After safely transporting the Royal train with H.R.H. Prince Philip to Hull, a pair of Stanier Black 5s sweep through Kelmarsh, returning the empty coaches to Wolverton carriage works on 18 May 1957. *(Ian L. Wright)*

205. A three coach local is easy work for the crew of Stanier 2-6-4 tank No. 42446, which is already feathering at the safety valves as the maximum boiler pressure of 200 p.s.i. is reached. This is a typically rural branch line scene at Kelmarsh, as the afternoon train prepares to depart towards Northampton during 1959. At this time No. 42446 was one of only four locomotives shedded at Market Harborough with the rare shed code 15F. *(Tony Heighton)*

Above: 206. The 3.45 p.m. Northampton to Market Harborough local train pulls smartly away from Clipston and Oxendon station, in the capable hands of Northampton-based Fowler 2-6-4 tank No. 42353 on Saturday, 18 April 1959, with Market Harborough being the next stop. *(Tony Heighton)*

Right: 207. Clipston and Oxendon station nameboard. *(Tony Heighton)*

208. There is a hive of activity at Market Harborough station on the night of 2 January 1960 as the clock approaches 10.15 p.m.

It is the last day of passenger services between Northampton and Market Harborough, and the final train should have left at 9.30 p.m. Ironically old Northampton faithful Ivatt tank No. 41218 had failed, which left local 'Super D' No. 49444 to shunt the stock into the station before disappearing into the night, leaving the passengers waiting around, steadily getting frozen in the process. To sighs of relief Fowler 2-6-4 tank No. 42331 appeared from out of the darkness, and connected up to the train. The relevant details are duly noted, with the train departing at 10.20 p.m. and arriving at Castle station at 10.59 p.m. The end of another eventful trip. (L. Hanson)

TOWARDS
THE WELLAND
VALLEY

NORTHAMPTON
TO MARKET
HARBOROUGH

209. Northampton veteran Webb 2-4-2 tank No. 46666 helps to pollute Market Harborough, as she awaits departure with the last train from Northampton to Melton Mowbray on 5 December 1953. No. 46666 is acting as pilot to an Ivatt 'Flying Pig', for the train of modern corridor coaches was thought to have been too much for the ageing veteran to pull alone.
(Ross Smith)

210. Lubenham station, which lies just outside the county boundary about two miles from Market Harborough, is one of the six stations situated along the Welland Valley from Rugby to Market Harborough. Rugby-based Stanier class 4 tank No. 42541 waits impatiently in the platform for departure time, with the Rugby to Market Harborough local train on Thursday, 9 July 1959. Although the station closed to goods traffic from 6 April 1964, passenger traffic continued for a further two years until 6 June 1966. *(Tony Heighton)*

TOWARDS THE WELLAND VALLEY

211. Fairburn class 4 tank No. 42061 from Rugby shed basks in the warm evening sunshine as it takes water, preparing to leave Market Harborough with the 7.25 p.m. local train to Northampton on Thursday, 9 July 1959. *(Tony Heighton)*

MARKET HARBOROUGH TO PETERBOROUGH

212. The points are set towards Nottingham for Burton-based 2P 4-4-0 No. 40436, standing in Luffenham station with a stopping passenger train from Peterborough on Saturday, 2 June 1951.

There would appear to be some sort of problem on the train as the station master and porter stride, stern faced, to investigate. The briefest glimpse of a W.D. 2-8-0 can be seen on the centre road. *(E. S. Russell)*

MARKET HARBOROUGH TO PETERBOROUGH

213. On the glorious summer Saturday of 2 June 1951, a local passenger train from Peterborough to Rugby drifts into Seaton station behind Johnson/Deeley Compound No. 41165. The fireman shouts across to a fellow engineman, whose Ivatt 2-6-2 tank No. 41278 stands at the head of its single-coach local train for Uppingham. In the distance another locomotive blows off impatiently, as it awaits clearance at the junction to proceed with its freight train in the same direction as 41165. (E. S. Russell)

Left: 214. Standard class 2 tank No. 84008 runs into the gloom of Morcott tunnel with a push-and-pull local train, the 10.20 a.m. Seaton to Stamford, on Saturday, 22 May 1965. On 4 October 1965 the Seaton to Stamford shuttle changed from steam to diesel; for its last week it had been the sole-surviving steam push and pull train in Britain! The line finally closed however on 6 June 1966, although the tunnel at Morcott still remains, as do the station buildings at Seaton. *(Derek Smith)*

Opposite: 215. Steam emanating from Standard 2-6-2 tank No. 84008 drifts around in the freezing winter air at Stamford Town station on Monday, 28 December 1964. The station staff have been busy snow clearing, in an effort to make conditions less hazardous for the passengers who have disembarked from this Seaton to Stamford local train. *(K. Fairey)*

TOWARDS THE WELLAND VALLEY

MARKET HARBOROUGH TO PETERBOROUGH

216. A Gresley V2 No. 60859 hurries over Walton level crossing on the East Coast main line, heading for Peterborough on Friday, 8 June 1962. Along this section, the Midland line from Peterborough ran parallel to the London and North Eastern, both being controlled by separate signal boxes and level crossings. In this view the signal box and open crossing gates are on the Midland line.

Shaded from the sun by his panama hat, the elderly gentleman passes the time of day watching the trains go by. He will have seen many changes since the early part of the century.
(P.I. Rawlinson)

217. Having traversed the East Coast main line via the M. and G.N.J.R. flyover, a train from South Lynn awaits clearance at the impressive ex-Midland thirteen-arm signal gantry, to enter Peterborough North station on Saturday, 9 August 1958. Gresley A3 Pacific No. 60063 ISINGLASS, the reason for the hold up, storms away from Westwood bridge with her northbound express, perfectly framed within the signal gantry. (P. I. Rawlinson)

THE ORIGINAL LINK

Left: 218. A summer Saturday in 1958 at Peterborough North station. Arrivals and departures come and go frequently, as normal express and local trains intersperse with the many additional holiday trains, providing the train spotters with a varied collection of numbers. In this view at the north end of the station a K3 class 'mogul' No. 61830 arrives with a local train, while V2 class No. 60855 waits to depart north with an express. On the left one of the ever present G.N.R. C12 class locomotives waits to continue duties as station pilot. *(Tony Heighton)*

Right: 219. Young and old stand and admire a magnificent Peppercorn A1 class Pacific No. 60130 KESTREL, as it rolls into platform 2 at Peterborough North station with a south-bound express, during the summer of 1960. To local railway enthusiasts a trip to Peterborough North via the East station was always an occasion to remember. A continuous stream of steam-hauled passenger and freight trains throughout the day, meant a chance to see locomotive numbers beginning with a '6' instead of the usual '4', and consequently numerous new additions to their notebooks. *(Tony Heighton)*

PETERBOROUGH TO BLISWORTH

220. Passengers prepare to board their train as Gresley A3 Pacific No. 60046 DIAMOND JUBILEE, recently outshopped with a double chimney, drifts into platform 2 at Peterborough North station with her express, bound for King's Cross, towards the end of 1958. In stations such as Peterborough North with an overall roof, the arrival and departure of trains always seemed spectacular and noisy. The steam and smoke drifting down from the roof provided a marvellous aroma to the steam enthusiast, but a dirty choking pollution to the normal traveller. *(B. Denny)*

221. One of the huge A5/1 class 4-6-2 tank locomotives No. 69803 proudly poses for the photographer at the south end of Peterborough North station, having just arrived with a local train from Boston on Saturday, 6 June 1953. The usual gathering of locospotters at the end of platform 3 endeavour to get nearer to the locomotive, to identify the unofficial name 'Sir Clem' that has been chalked onto the smokebox. Originally designed by Robinson on the Great Central in 1911, thirty of these locomotives were built between 1911 and 1923. From 1925 to 1926 a further thirteen A5/2 class were built, with slight differences designed by Gresley. *(Ian L. Wright)*

THE ORIGINAL LINK

222. On 11 September 1938, the very first R.C.T.S. organised tour ran as a return trip from Kings Cross to Peterborough. To re-create travel from times past Patrick Stirlings 'Single' No. 1 was loaned from York Railway Museum to haul the train, and a search was made for some six-wheel Great Northern carriages. Eventually seven were located, and these were re-painted to represent East Coast Joint stock. The combination looked superb, and was photographed many times throughout its journey. Here we see crowds that have gathered to witness the spectacle on its arrival at Peterborough North. (L. Hanson)

223. Special tickets were printed for the half-day excursion, the photographer's being No. 45. (L. Hanson)

PETERBOROUGH TO BLISWORTH

224. A Victorian-built 'old stager' ex-G.N.R. class C12 No. 67357 of 1898 vintage, brings a rake of empty coaches from the Nene carriage sidings and approaches Peterborough North station on Tuesday, 8 April 1958. No. 67357 was one of six C12 class locomotives to be shedded at New England during 1958, and all were withdrawn at the end of that year; one of the last duties for the class was to work on the Essendine to Stamford branch line. In the background the fine iron arched road bridge crosses the Great Northern main line and the beginning of 'south yard' on the left. *(Tony Heighton)*

Above: 225. A panoramic view, fairly typical of the branch, taken in September 1963, showing a B1 pulling away from Irthlingborough station with a Peterborough to Northampton local. *(Ian L. Wright)*

Left: 226. Shrouded in leaking steam, the shunter discusses tactics with the crew of ex-Great Central J11 0-6-0 No. 64288, at Irthlingborough station on a chilly December day in 1952. The station canopies are still in wartime grey paint, and on the station wall of the down platform the large '20' sign indicates 20 miles from Blisworth, starting point of the original link with Peterborough. At this time there was still a wagon turntable in use at the goods yard, on which wagons could be turned at right angles to enter the goods warehouse. *(Ian L. Wright)*

Opposite top: 227. The people of Wellingborough go about their business and generally pass the time of day, in the vicinity of London Road station during June 1935. *(W. J. S. Meredith)*

Opposite bottom: 228. This view, photographed from the footbridge at London Road station, shows a Fowler 4F 0-6-0 No. 44340 taking the curve towards the Midland main line and Corby, hauling its freight on Monday, 5 December 1960. The back end of the train can be seen adjacent to the platform. *(Ian L. Wright)*

Above: 229. Wellingborough-based Standard tank class 2 No. 84008 makes a spirited afternoon departure from Wellingborough London Road station, pushing its two coaches, with a local push-pull train to Northampton from the Midland Road station during November 1959. One of the main duties of the signalman in the London Road signal box was to control the gates on the busy level crossing, which was situated at the junction of the A45 and A509 roads into Wellingborough, and adjacent to the station. *(Tony Heighton)*

230. A bird's eye view of Northampton from over Delapre Park on Wednesday, 13 May 1959, shows an interesting panorama of the town. At Cotton End traffic queues at the level crossing gates as the 4.02 p.m. train to Bedford prepares to leave Bridge Street station behind an Ivatt 2-6-2 tank, while in the goods yard (bottom right) an ex-Midland 3F shunts the yards (almost certainly No. 43399, as it was the only member of the class at Northampton

THE ORIGINAL LINK

in 1959). It is interesting to note that none of the town centre modernisation has yet started; the Emporium Arcade, Newland, the Old Brewery and even part of St. John's Street station, remain intact. Another interesting feature, usually only seen by those who attended, is the Greyhound Stadium (bottom right). *(Aerofilms Ltd.)*

PETERBOROUGH TO BLISWORTH

231. One of Francis Webb's Jubilee class four cylinder compound 4-4-0s No. 1932 ANSON provides the stage for a photograph at Northampton Locomotive Shed circa 1912.

Local railwaymen Beasley, Dimmock, Lake, Ling and Watts are among the group taking a short break from their work. A day which began at 6 a.m. and finished at 5.30 p.m., during which time there was a welcome one-hour break for dinner.

(Keith Adams Collection)

232. Having come off the shed road, 'Baby Scot' No. 5522 PRESTATYN drifts under the bridge carrying the Northampton to Roade line during 1947. After passing Duston West signal box she will cross over and reverse round the curve on the far left, to pick up her train at Castle station. The headlamp code indicates the train to be a local passenger, probably a stopping train to Euston. PRESTATYN stayed in this original form until January 1949, before being rebuilt with a large Stanier type 2A taper boiler. (R. Gammage)

233. Old Northampton faithful, Ivatt tank No. 41218 in a familiar role at bay platform 4, waits to depart with a special working to Blisworth on Easter Sunday, 17 April 1955. She is due out at 11.51 a.m., to connect with a diverted Wolverhampton to Euston express. *(Ross Smith)*

M 475

L·M·S
LONDON MIDLAND AND SCOTTISH RAILWAY.

AN OPPORTUNITY TO VISIT THE NEW BLISWORTH LIDO.

ON

Sundays, September 17th & 24th

the following Special Trains will run to

BLISWORTH

FROM		Times of Departure.				RETURN FARES Third Class
		p.m.	p.m.	p.m.	p.m.	
Northampton (Castle) ... dep.		3 0	5 0	7 10	9 10	-/8
Roade .... „		3 15	5 15	7 25	9 25	-/5
		p.m.	p.m.	p.m.	p.m.	
Blisworth .... arr.		3 20	5 20	7 35	9 30	

RETURNING AS UNDER:—

	p.m.	p.m.	p.m.	p.m.
Blisworth ....dep.	4 0	6 0	8 35	10 25
Roade .... „	4 10	6 10	8 45	10 35
Northampton .... arr.	4 20	6 20	8 57	10 46

Children under three years of age, Free ; three years and under fourteen, Half-fares.

LUGGAGE ALLOWANCE.

Passengers holding Day or Half-day Excursion Tickets are not allowed to take any luggage except small handbags, luncheon baskets or other small articles intended for the passenger's use during the day. On the return journey only passengers may take with them, free of charge at owner's risk, goods for their own use not exceeding 60 lbs.

The Blisworth Lido is situated in the beautiful Blisworth Hotel grounds, comprising 8 acres of glorious woodland scenery.

Admission to grounds (including Bathing fee) 1/-

Tickets and Bills can be obtained at the Stations, and from the following LMS Railway Agencies :—
NORTHAMPTON—Messrs. FRAMES' TOURS, LTD., 11, Gold Street, Northampton. Tel. 530.
„ Messrs. PICKFORDS' LTD., 7, Wood Hill, Northampton. Tel. 1449.

Conditions of Issue of Excursion and other Reduced Fare Tickets.
Excursion Tickets, and Tickets issued at Fares less than the Ordinary Fares, are issued subject to the Notices and Conditions shewn in the Company's current Time Tables.

All information regarding Excursion Trains on the London Midland and Scottish Railway may be obtained on application to the L M S Stations or Agencies, or to Mr. H. W. EDE, District Goods and Passenger Manager, Castle Station, Northampton.

September, 1933.   **ASHTON DAVIES, Chief Commercial Manager.**
(E.R.O.53302)

(3,500)   McCorquodale & Co., Ltd. Printers, London and Newton.—1742   M 475

234. A 1933 publicity handout advertising special train workings, to visit the new Blisworth lido. *(L. Hanson)*

THE ORIGINAL LINK
PETERBOROUGH TO BLISWORTH

Left: 235. A pleasant autumnal afternoon by the side of the Grand Union canal at Northampton locomotive shed on Saturday, 21 October 1961. Locomotives have already gathered for their weekend rest, no doubt to be followed by a few others before the end of the day, in readiness for the trainspotters the next day. *(L. W. Roy)*

Below: 236. Looking back towards the shed from the canal lock gates, Ivatt tank No. 41219 propels its push-and-pull from Blisworth, round the tight curve towards Castle station, in the autumn of 1956. *(P. I. Rawlinson)*

Opposite top: 238. The sun falls to the horizon, bringing to an end a beautiful summer's day on Thursday, 7 June 1962. It is just bright enough though to witness the passage of Stanier Jubilee No. 45552 SILVER JUBILEE, doyen of her class, heading towards Blisworth at 9.10 p.m., hauling a Wolverhampton to Euston express. *(R. A. F. Puryer)*

Above: 237. The 10 to 2 or 'Llandudno' heads for London via Blisworth, running an hour late behind Stanier Coronation Pacific No. 46253 CITY OF ST. ALBANS, on Saturday, 29 September 1962. The signal box was unusual in having two names, 'Duston West' at high level controlling the line to Roade, and 'Duston Junction West' at low level controlling the Blisworth line. *(R. A. F. Puryer)*

THE ORIGINAL LINK
PETERBOROUGH TO BLISWORTH

Opposite bottom: 239. Reduced to using coal briquettes and wood owing to the coal strike, Bowen-Cooke George the Fifth No. 1623 NUBIAN and Claughton No. 2427, cruise effortlessly through Blisworth station with the 11.05 express from Liverpool on Saturday, 30 April 1921. No. 2427 received the name DUKE OF CONNAUGHT the following January. Re-numbered No. 5946 by the L.M.S., it was rebuilt with large boiler and Caprotti valve gear in August 1928, surviving in that form until February 1941. No. 1623 was re-numbered No. 5364 and survived until November 1936. Both locomotives are in L.N.W.R. lined black livery, with a various assortment of rolling stock in plum and spilt milk. The reason for having such a tall signal, was so that the driver could sight it over the top of the previous bridge, thus giving him more time to act should it be necessary. *(L. J. Thompson)*

S.M.J. TO G.W.R.

240. Typical view of the rural charm associated with the Stratford-upon-Avon and Midland Junction Railway. An ex-Midland 3F No. 3767, of Stratford shed, idles away time standing at Blisworth with its two wagon loads of cattle, in the summer of 1947. The driver and fireman have obviously found an interest completely devoid of railway matters, which appears to have been fairly typical on the S.M.J., where rabbiting, mushrooming and various other activities were fairly commonplace. From the people spoken to, great enjoyment was had by all those fortunate enough to have worked on the line.
(R. J. Rawlinson)

Above: 241. Although the S.M.J. terminated at Ravenstone Wood Junction, it had running powers over the Midland line to Olney, some three and a half miles distance. In 'The Field' opposite the station the Midland railway provided turntable, shed and watering facilities for the use of locomotives coming off the S.M.J. On Saturday, 29 June 1957 Bedford 4F No. 44317, having arrived on a freight from Towcester, waits to be turned on the fifty feet diameter turntable. Later in the day she will pilot a return freight to Towcester and Stratford-upon-Avon. The 9,000 gallon water tower still stands, but the wooden single road engine shed *(top right)* was demolished in the late 1930s. *(K. Fairey)*

Right: 242. The forty feet diameter S.M.J. turntable at Blisworth is barely large enough to accommodate Fowler 4F No. 44061, and it's 'shoulders to it', as the crew slowly swing her round during a summer afternoon in 1958. *(B. Denny)*

Above/left: 243/244. Wartime demand for iron ore meant the opening of more quarries. Blisworth Mines was created in 1942, when a substantial financial outlay was invested in the building of the standard gauge system, about a mile in length, from the junction with the former S.M.J. to the quarry. It was 1945 when Richard Thomas and Baldwins Ltd. became the owners, by which time iron ore production had ceased. However, by the late 1950s production began again, and lasted for about twelve years until 1969. The views in these pictures show 'Ettrick', an 0-4-0ST, built by Hawthorn Leslie in 1928, standing outside the locomotive shed at the end of a morning shift in the spring of 1967. The engine had arrived in May 1957, and was the last working locomotive on the system. *(Joe Rajczonek)*

Right: 245. The peace and tranquillity of the S.M.J. is summed up in this photograph at Towcester, taken on a balmy summer's day in 1939, a typical everyday scene. None of the hustle and bustle as found on the main lines, just an ex-Midland 2F casually easing some wagons into the sidings at the eastern end of the station. There were odd times however, during Towcester horse racing days, when special trains arrived and caused a temporary spell of activity in the station. *(W.J.S. Meredith)*

S.M.J. TO G.W.R.: STRATFORD-UPON-AVON AND MIDLAND JUNCTION RAILWAY

Opposite: 246. Under the impressive array of signals at the western end of Towcester station, an ex-Midland 2F shunts the sidings on the opposite side of the Watling Street (A5) during the same summer day in 1939. The two lines going out over the bridge were both worked single line, the one on the left being for trains to and from Banbury, and the right to and from Stratford-upon-Avon. Care had to be taken when using the 41′ 9″ diameter turntable, otherwise the locomotive would probably have ended up on Watling Street. *(W. J. S. Meredith)*

Right: 247. The very small booking hall at Byfield station photographed in March 1965, thirteen years after passenger services ceased on 7 April 1952, and just after the withdrawal of goods traffic from Byfield ironstone sidings. *(P. I. Rawlinson)*

Below: 248. Northampton Fowler 4F No. 44353 eases through Byfield station, as her crew give out some good natured banter to the signalman as they pick up the staff circa 1960. The 4F can now proceed towards Towcester and Blisworth with her local pick-up freight. *(Tony Heighton)*

Left: 249. Ex-Midland 3F 0-6-0 No. 3594 draws up at Cockley Brake Junction, with her fireman ready to exchange the single line staff on Saturday, 15 May 1948. From this lonely outpost she will be heading on to the S.M.J. branch line towards Towcester and Blisworth, with her single coach passenger train. *(E. S. Russell)*

Opposite top: 250. The entrance to Banbury Merton Street station, on a wet and dismal day towards the end of the 1950s. *(Tony Heighton)*

Opposite bottom: 251. Ex-Midland 3F 0-6-0 No. 3594 has more than enough steam, as she awaits departure time from Banbury Merton Street station with the afternoon train for Blisworth on Saturday, 15 May 1948. A substantial amount of cattle freight emanated from the large cattle market situated adjacent to the station, with trains departing via Blisworth, Bletchley and the Great Western exchange sidings to various points of the country. *(E. S. Russell)*

S.M.J. TO G.W.R.
STRATFORD-UPON-AVON AND MIDLAND JUNCTION RAILWAY

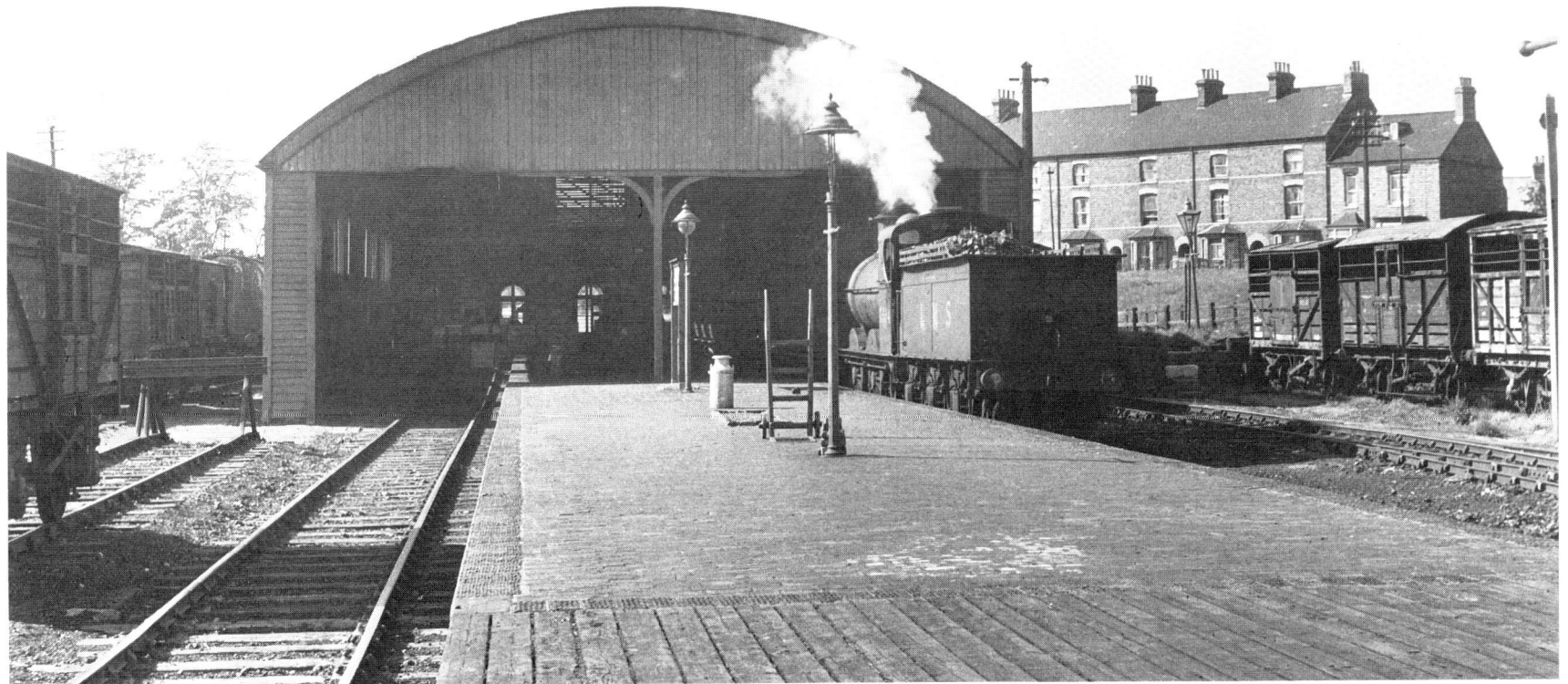

252. Banbury station on a summer Saturday in August 1960. County class No. 1003 COUNTY OF WILTS has arrived on an inter-regional train from the Southern Region, with a full complement of Southern Region coaches. Another number goes into the trainspotters book, as the northbound express brews up ready for a prompt departure. (L. W. Roy)

S.M.J. TO G.W.R.
GREAT WESTERN RAILWAY

Opposite: 253. On 24 May 1962 the Royal Train, with Her Majesty the Queen on board, arrived at Banbury from Wolverhampton behind Castle class 4-6-0 No. 4082 WINDSOR CASTLE. As the train will be spending the night on a branch near Adderbury, the Castle has been replaced by Manor class 4-6-0s No. 7817 GARSINGTON MANOR and No. 7824 IFORD MANOR. Here the two gleaming Manors storm away from the south end of Banbury station, past a group of admiring trainspotters and head for the branch. The locomotives will provide steam heating for the stationary train, while a third Manor, hauling a service train, will travel from Adderbury station bringing water to replenish tanks, and two tons of wet ice for the air conditioning system of the Royal Saloons. (K. Fairey)

S.M.J. TO G.W.R.: GREAT WESTERN RAILWAY

Oppposite: 254. This delightful scene, taken during the summer of 1956, shows Banbury based Pannier tank No. 5424 (one of 25 built with 5′ 2″ wheels for Auto-train work) at Aynho Park station with a Banbury to Bicester local train. Although reminiscent of a branch line scene, the line is in fact the Great Western and Great Central Joint, and was the last main line steam railway to be built in England. Aynho Park, which opened on 1 July 1910, was one of two stations serving Aynho and its great house. The older station was on the Oxford to Banbury line nearby, and was called 'Aynho for Deddington'. Aynho Park finally closed on 7 January 1963. (*C. Lucas*)

Above: 255. Banbury shedded Hall class No. 6929 WHORLTON HALL heads south through King's Sutton station with the 8.55 a.m. Sheffield (Victoria) to Bournemouth (Central) on Saturday, 8 September 1962. In previous years this train would have travelled along the Great Central route. The Great Western station opened in 1872, and at one time the village had illusions of becoming a Spa. The spring of mineral water was situated near the railway within a railed enclosure and the waters were said to have a taste equal to Leamington's. The station lost its staff from 2 November 1964, and was renamed King's Sutton Halt on 6 May 1968. (*R. A. F. Puryer*)

256. Low winter lighting has created this dramatic scene of Grange class No. 6803 BUCKLEBURY GRANGE, approaching King's Sutton station with a northbound goods train on the morning of Saturday, 8 February 1964. In the background the bridge, carry-ing the Chipping Norton branch line over the River Cherwell and Oxford Canal, marks the county boundary. The Oxley (Wolverhampton) based locomotive was finally withdrawn in September 1965. *(R. A. F. Puryer)*

GREAT WESTERN RAILWAY

257. The southern approach to King's Sutton station offers a superb rural view of the Great Western Railway running through the Northamptonshire countryside. Hall class No. 5953 DUNLEY HALL shatters the tranquility of a perfect summer's afternoon, with the 9.11 a.m. Eastbourne to Wolverhampton (via Kensington Olympia) train hauling a rake of Southern coaches on Saturday, 8 September 1962. The locomotive was also withdrawn from service the following month. The branch line going off to the right is the King's Sutton to Chipping Norton, which closed to traffic two years later on 7 September 1964. (R. A. F. Puryer)

258. Steaming into Northamptonshire in 1988! Steam excursions can still regularly be seen coming through the county between Aynho and King's Sutton, with trains from both Didcot and Marylebone to Banbury and beyond. In this winter's view A4 class ex-L.N.E.R. Pacific No. 4498 SIR NIGEL GRESLEY streaks past King's Sutton village with an excursion to Sheffield. The superb spire of the fourteenth century church of St. Peter and St. Paul dominates the landscape, and is probably the finest example in Northamptonshire, a county famous for its many spires.
(Joe Rajczonek)

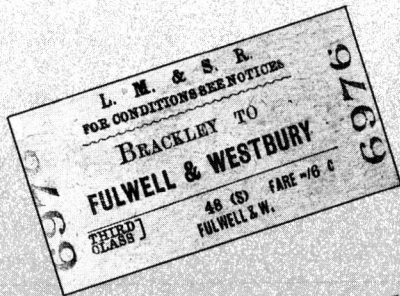

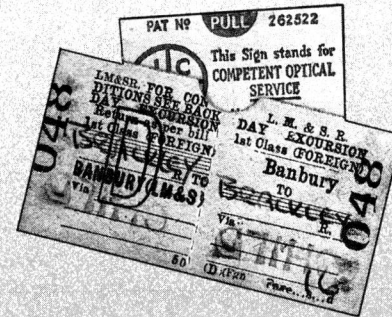

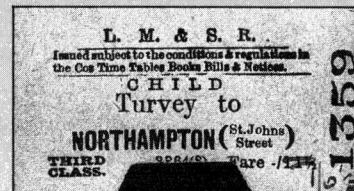

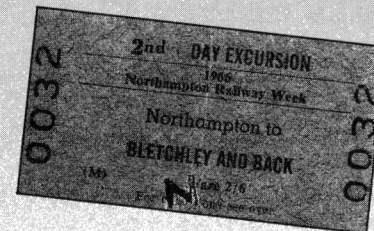

259. Ticket collector Miss Nichols at Wellingborough, London Road station, probably during the First World War.
(*T. Sharp, courtesy of G. Stewart*)

Above and overleaf: 260. In January 1931 the L.M.S. introduced railway tickets with advertising inserts that slotted into the top of the ticket. The revenue earned from this went a long way towards covering the cost of production. This selection of local railway tickets is made up using examples from the collections of *Tony Heighton, Peter Butler, Les Hanson and Ron Gammage.*

Corot — buy your next outfit from corot / 55 old bond st, london / models, frocks, co... / CONDITIONS SEE BACK / L.M.S.R. 0840 TO / BRIXWORTH K. / LAMPORT / TO AL... / Via / 7S (S)(Fgn) FARE / 1st CLASS (FOREIGN)

2nd FORCES LEAVE SINGLE / 0001 Clipston & Oxendon to KELMARSH / Via / For alternative routes see book of routes / (M) 3 FARE / For conditions see over / 0001

2nd · SINGLE SINGLE · 2nd / 0179 CHILD / Kelmarsh to / Kelmarsh Market Harborough Kelmarsh / Market Harborough Market Harborough / MARKET HARBOROUGH CHILD / (M) 0/5 Fare 0/5 (M) / For conditions see over For conditions see over / 0179

3rd · SINGLE / 0609 Kettering to / GRETTON or MARKET HARBOROUGH CHILD / (M) FARE 1/03 / For conditions see over / 0609

3rd · SINGLE SINGLE · 3rd / Glendon & Rushton To / Glendon & Rushton Glendon & Rushton / Desborough & Desborough & / Rothwell Rothwell / DESBOROUGH & ROTHWELL / 9771 (M) 0/6 Fare 0/6 (M) 9771 / For conditions see over For conditions see over

2nd · SPECIAL CHEAP DAY SPECIAL CHEAP DAY · 2nd / 0035 Glendon & Rushton t KETTERING / Kettering to GLENDON & RUSHTON / (M) Fare 0/11 Fare 0/11 (M) / For conditions see over For conditions see over / 0035

2nd · CHEAP DAY CHEAP DAY · 2nd / 1213 Kettering to THRAPSTON (Mid Rd.) / Thrapston (Mid Rd.) to KETTERING / (M) Fare 2/3 Fare 2/3 (M) / For conditions see over For conditions see over / 1213

PAT. NO. PULL 262522 / SEE YOUR DENTIST TWICE A YEAR / Issued by B. L.M. & S.R. / L.M.S.R. FOR CONDITIONS SEE BACK / Available for 1st Class (FOREIGN) 1st Class (FOREIGN) / RAUNDS R.To Thrapton (M.Rd) / THRAPSTON (M.RD) R.To RAUNDS / Via Via / 0619 149R Fgn. Fare 2s 0d 0619

076 L.M. & S.R. FOR CONDITIONS SEE NOTICES / Irchester to WELLINGBORO / Via RLY. / FIRST CLASS 3860 (S Fare 1/1 / 076

3rd HALF DAY EXCURSION HALF DAY EXCURSION 3rd / 6158 Northampton (Castle) to RUSHDEN / Rushden TO NORTHAMPTON (Castle) / (M) Fare 2/6 Fare 2/6 (M) / For conditions see over For conditions see over / 6150

2nd · SINGLE SINGLE · 2nd / 1963 Higham Ferrers to / Higham Ferrers Higham Ferrers / Rushden Rushden / RUSHDEN / (M) 0/2 FARE 0/2 (M) / For conditions see over For conditions see over / 1963

L.M. & S.R. for conditions see notices L.M. & S.R. / 177 MONTHLY RET. MONTHLY RET. / valid advertised THIRD CLASS / THIRD CLASS / Irthlingboro' Ringstead &A / TO TO / RINGSTEAD & A IRTHLINGBORO' / Fare 7½C Fare 8½ / 8R (MR) IRTHLINGBORO 177

INDEX OF LOCOMOTIVES: ALL BRITISH RAILWAYS NUMBERS UNLESS STATED

Numbers in italics are illustration numbers

KEY TO LETTERS INCORPORATED IN LOCOMOTIVE CLASS NUMBERS

P = Passenger
F = Freight
MT = Mixed Traffic (i.e. passenger/freight)
* = Rebuilt with larger boiler
† = Rebuilt with larger tapered boiler

Fowler 'Royal Scot' class 6P, 7P 4-6-0 introduced 1927
† 46100 ROYAL SCOT, *201*
L.M.S. No. 6105 CAMERON HIGHLANDER, *25*
† 46122 ROYAL ULSTER RIFLEMAN, *84*
† 46123 ROYAL IRISH FUSILIER, *94*
† 46129 THE SCOTTISH HORSE, *18*
† 46132 THE KING'S REGIMENT, LIVER-POOL, *68*
† 46133 THE GREEN HOWARDS, *87*
L.M.S. No. 6140 HECTOR, *23*
† 46140 THE KING'S ROYAL RIFLE CORPS, *17*
L.M.S. No. 6147 THE NORTHAMPTONSHIRE REGIMENT, *160, 161*
† 46148 THE MANCHESTER REGIMENT, *17*

Stanier 'Princess Royal' class 8P 4-6-2 introduced 1933
L.M.S. No. 6202, *180*
L.M.S. No. 6206 PRINCESS MARIE LOUISE, *Title page, 182*
46207 PRINCESS ARTHUR OF CONNAUGHT, *34, 35*
46209 PRINCESS BEATRICE, *16*

Stanier 'Coronation' class 8P 4-6-2 introduced 1937
46221 QUEEN ELIZABETH, *176*
46226 DUCHESS OF NORFOLK, *47*
46231 DUCHESS OF ATHOLL, *177*
46234 DUCHESS OF ABERCORN, *24*
46246 CITY OF MANCHESTER, *178*
46253 CITY OF ST. ALBANS, *237*

Ivatt 'Mogul' class 2MT 2-6-0 introduced 1946
46404, *126*
46444, *105, 131*
46496, *125, 128, 129*

Fowler 'Jinty' class 3F 0-6-0 Tank introduced 1924
47273, *88*
47543, *88*
L.M.S. No. 7554, *85*

Beyer-Garratt class 2-6-0-0-6-2 introduced 1927
(freight) 47980, *90*
47994, *79*

Stanier class 8F 2-8-0 introduced 1935
48008, *36*
48069, *119*
48163, *190*
48177, *96, 100*
48194, *179*
48290, *60*
48332, *172*
48381, *97, 104*
48530, *96*
48544, *194*
48554, *193*
48603, *189*
48614, *88*
48625, *88*
48635, *108*

L.N.E.R.
Gresley streamlined 'A4' class 8P 4-6-2 introduced 1935
L.N.E.R. No. 4498 SIR NIGEL GRESLEY, *258*

Gresley 'A3' class 7P 4-6-2 introduced 1927
60046 DIAMOND JUBILEE, *220*
60063 ISINGLASS, *217*
60107 ROYAL LANCER, *51*

Peppercorn 'A1' class 8P 4-6-2 introduced 1948
60130 KESTREL, *219*

Gresley 'V2' class 6MT 2-6-2 introduced 1936
60828, *54*
60855, *218*
60859, *216*
60879, *65*
60890, *52*
60982, *58*

Thompson 'B1' class 5MT 4-6-0 introduced 1942
61044, *53*

Gresley 'B16/2' class 6MT 4-6-0 introduced 1937 (original design by Raven in 1920)
61455, *66*

Gresley 'K3/2' class 6MT 2-6-0 introduced 1924
61830, *218*

Gresley D16/3 class 3P 4-4-0 introduced 1936 (original design by Holden in 1904)
62535, *159*

Thompson 'O1' class 8F 2-8-0 introduced 1944 (original design by Robinson in 1911)
63725, *78*

Thompson 'L1' class 4MT 2-6-4 Tank introduced 1945
67789, *56*

G.C.R.
Pollitt '11A' class 4-4-0 introduced 1897 *(passenger)*
G.C. No. 270, *63*

Robinson 'J11' class 3F 0-6-0 introduced 1901
64288, *226*

Robinson 'A5/1' class 4P 4-6-2 Tank introduced 1911
69803, *221*

G.E.R.
Worsdell 'J15' class 2F 0-6-0 introduced 1883
65461, *124*
65475, *130*

G.N.R.
Stirling single class 4-2-2 introduced 1870 *(passenger)*
G.N. No. 1, *222*

Ivatt 'C12' class 2P 4-4-2 Tank introduced 1898
67357, *224*

B.R.
Riddles 'Britannia' class 7P 4-6-2 introduced 1951
70004 WILLIAM SHAKESPEARE, *81*
70015 APOLLO, *80*
70034 THOMAS HARDY, *33*

Riddles Standard class 5MT 4-6-0 introduced 1951
73045, *55*

Riddles Standard Caprotti class 5MT 4-6-0 introduced 1956
73142, *91*
73144, *111*

Riddles Standard class 4MT 4-6-0 introduced 1951
75052, *169*

Riddles Standard class 2MT 2-6-0 introduced 1952
78020, *127*

Riddles Standard class 2MT 2-6-2 Tank introduced 1953
84005, *148*
84006, *143, 175*
84007, *141, 142, 198*
84008, *214, 215, 229*

Riddles Standard class 9F 2-10-0 introduced 1954
92056, *74*
92093, *50*
92104, *95*
92112, *101*
92154, *195*
92160, *81*
92163, *187*

LIST OF ABBREVIATIONS

B.R.	British Railways
G.C.R.	Great Central Railway
G.E.R.	Great Eastern Railway
G.N.R.	Great Northern Railway
G.W.R.	Great Western Railway
L.M.S.	London Midland and Scottish Railway
L.N.E.R.	London and North Eastern Railway
L.N.W.R.	London and North Western Railway
L.&Y.R.	Lancashire and Yorkshire Railway
M.&G.N.J.R.	Midland and Great Northern Joint Railway
M.R.	Midland Railway
S.M.J.	Stratford-upon-Avon and Midland Junction Railway

INDUSTRIAL LOCOMOTIVES

Builder / LOCO NAME/NUMBER	TYPE	CYLINDER	MAKER'S NO.	YEAR BUILT	GAUGE	
Avonside Engine Co. Ltd.						
HARTINGTON	0-6-0ST	OC	1869	1921	Standard	*199*
Black, Hawthorn & Co. Ltd.						
KETTERING FURNACES No. 2	0-4-0ST	OC	501	1879	3' 0"	*114, 115*
Hawthorn Leslie & Co. Ltd						
ETTRICK	0-4-0ST	OC	3721	1928	Standard	*243, 244*
No. 16	0-6-0ST	OC	3837	1934	Standard	*118*
Manning Wardle & Co. Ltd.						
KETTERING FURNACES No. 7	0-6-0ST	OC	1370	1897	3' 0"	*113*
KETTERING FURNACES No. 8	0-6-0ST	OC	1675	1906	3' 0"	*113*
Peckett & Sons Ltd.						
LAMPORT	0-6-0ST	OC	1315	1913	3' 0"	*200*
Robert Stephenson & Hawthorns Ltd.						
No. 57	0-6-0ST	1C	7668	1950	Standard	*116*

County of Northampton

THE NORTHAMPTONSHIRE REGIMENT 6147 L M S